Southampton People

Eminent Sotonians and Assorted Characters

Southampton People

Eminent Sotonians and Assorted Characters

John Edgar Mann

Ensign
PUBLICATIONS

Published in 1989 by
Ensign Publications
2 Redcar St
Southampton, SO1 5LL

Designed and typeset by Robert Anthony Limited, Ringwood.
Edited by David Graves.

ISBN 1 85455 021 7

ENSIGN PUBLICATIONS
SOUTHAMPTON

British Library Cataloguing in Publication Data
Mann, John Edgar 1928
    Southampton people: eminent Sotonians and assorted characters.
    1. Hampshire, Southampton. Biographies. Collections.
    I. Title
    942.2'76'0922

ISBN 1 85455 021 7

The Author

John Edgar Mann was born in Thornhill Park Road in 1928 and, apart from a wartime spell at school in Bournemouth, has lived in Southampton all his life. Until his retirement in 1988 he had worked for 42 years on the local evening newspaper, the *Echo*, in various editorial capacities — office boy, reporter, sub-editor, cinema and theatre critic, features editor and finally columnist on the Tom Bargate page.

His interests, apart from local history, include movies old and new, jazz and folk music (he is a past-chairman of Southampton Rhythm Club and for 20 years was secretary of the city's Fo'c'sle Folk Music Club).

This is his second book. His first, Southampton Past and Present, was published in 1985.

INTRODUCTION

The interesting people whose stories are told in these pages divide into three categories: those who were born in Southampton, stayed and made an impression on the place; those who first saw the light of day in it but who chose to seek their fortunes elsewhere; and those non-natives who were happy to adopt Southampton as their home town (or, in one case, port) and make a contribution to it.

There are heroes and heroines here, certainly, but one or two clay-footed personalities too — just the same as in any community. One quality they all shared, or share: talent, whether in the realms of war or business, art or architecture, literature or music, politics or science, entertainment or sport. "Sotonians" (and the inventor of that word is here too) will be proud to acknowledge most of them as fellow citizens.

Inevitably I will be criticised for omitting people. I plead guilty, my defence being that what you hold in your hands represents only a selection.

Finally, some acknowledgements. Sir Christopher Cockerell made several constructive biographical suggestions; John Carr gladly provided me with tape-recorded reminiscences by his father, C. F. Carr; Nat Gonella was good enough to fill in some gaps in my knowledge of his Southampton years; Captain John Treasure Jones generously set aside an afternoon of his retirement to talk to me; Mrs. Wyn Pitcher and "Nobby" Reid helped me greatly concerning the life of their brother, Billy (thanks also to the scores of people who rang or wrote following a newspaper appeal on the subject of the prolific composer); Peter Munro, acting principal of Richard Taunton College, kindly provided me with a portrait of the founder; and Jasmine Profit, to whom this book is dedicated, added to my knowledge of General Shrapnel.

I thank my old paper the *Echo,* whose librarian, Peter Ashton, proved endlessly patient with my inquiries, for permission to use their photographs. Malcolm Nethersole, of the Echo photographic department, helped me greatly, and local historian Alan Leonard was, as always, ready and willing with his assistance.

J.E.M.

CONTENTS

CONTENTS

Richard Andrews

The good man who has been termed "Southampton's Dick Whittington" certainly had a lot in common with the pantomime hero who was called back to London by the Bow bells. According to legend, Dick — accompanied by his devoted cat — walked back to a beckoning fortune and became Mayor of London four times.

Richard Andrews, too, walked to the town where he would make his fortune. Though there is no record of a feline companion in his case, he was one up on the 15th century Richard by becoming Mayor of Southampton five times.

Southampton's Dick Whittington was born at Bishop's Sutton, near Alresford, in 1798. His only education was at a dame's school for twopence a week, and that was only for three or four years. At nine he was a threepence-a-week farm boy. Then he had a job in a sawmill at Itchenstoke — which entailed a daily ten-mile walk — before serving his time as a blacksmith.

In 1822, though newly wed, he set off on the walk to Southampton, with only half a crown in his pocket, and found employment with a coachmaker. Ten years later, bolstered by his savings of £75, he set up in his own coachmaking business in Above Bar. By 1845 he was employing 200 men and earning the then gigantic sum of £20,000 a year.

Though the coming of the railways, of course, adversely affected carriage-making, Richard didn't suffer too badly — he had wisely built up a big export trade to many countries. But for all his wealth, Richard Andrews seems to have been a good employer who "devoted himself wholeheartedly to promoting the self-reliance of the working man."

So states the modern plaque beneath the statue of Andrews in East Park. This memorial, which has led generations of Sotonians to refer to East Park as Andrews' Park (just as its neighbour, West Park, is popularly dubbed Watts Park), now looks sadly depleted.

The original memorial by Andrews' fellow Liberal Philip Brannon, the architect-artist-inventor who appears elsewhere in this book, was a typically ornate and grandiose Victorian affair put up by popular subscription after the coachbuilder's death on March 28, 1859. A memorial committee considered five designs and, after some demurring by a sub-committee, elected to select Brannon's by

The memorial to Richard Andrews, considerably reduced in size and splendour and minus a nose.

Southampton's Dick Whittington

11 votes to three. Stone carver Benjamin Brain from Shirley set to work and the foundation stone was laid on October 1, 1860.

This date, as was pointed out at the time, was highly appropriate, for it was on October 1, 1832, that Richard Andrews began his career as a tradesman in Southampton . . . a day when, said Sheriff Weston, "he was wont for many years to assemble round his hospitable board his employees and friends."

The measure of Andrews' popularity can be gained by comtemporary reports of the ceremony. We read that, after a civic procession from the Audit House to "East Marlands Common Field", a crowd of 4,000 assembled to see the stone laid by the Mayor, Frederick Perkins.

The Bath stone used for the elaborate memorial failed to resist weathering and in 1971 the pedestal had to be taken down. The statue itself, never much admired, now looks more unimpressive than ever — in fairness, Brannon intended it to be looked up to, 12 to 15 feet above eye level.

The pedestal originally acclaimed "a man who, starting from small beginnings, achieved by the force of his own genius solid triumphs, civic rank, popularity and fame — the rewards of industry, public spirit and hospitality." Another inscription read: "The life of Richard Andrews teaches us this lesson: that the merit of a man is in himself, not in his calling. He may be engaged in trade, yet be great: he may have worn the apron of an artisan, yet live to win a patriot's monument."

Richard Andrews, a man who never feared expressing political convictions unpopular with most of his clients, left to his son Arthur a silver salver presented to him by his fellow townsmen

Richard Andrews, from a painting (artist unknown) in Southampton Art Gallery.

for his advocacy of the repeal of the Corn Laws . . . "a measure," he said in his will, "which has so much contributed to give the poor man a larger loaf and to cheapen the necessary provisions of life for the benefit of all."

Arthur also got a silver candelabra presented to his father "on the defeat of a measure relating to the imposition of a rate on small tenements, which appeared to me oppressive and unjust." The Nonconformist Richard Andrews, it's obvious, was a chap who really practised his Christianity. . . .

11

Jane Austen

T hough a resident of Southampton for less than three years, Jane Austen nevertheless knew the place well. She had been at school in the town for a short time and danced at a ball there when she was 18. And then, from the summer of 1806 until the spring of 1809, she shared a house in Castle Square with her mother, sister, sailor brother Frank, his new bride, and a friend named Martha Lloyd.

Alas, no fiction came from Jane during these years, which fell between the publication of *Sense and Sensibility* and *Mansfield Park,* but those Austen gifts described by Arthur Compton-Rickett in his History of English Literature — "faithful observation, personal detachment, and a fine sense of ironic comedy" — failed to desert her.

When Jane and her brother Captain Frank Austen, RN, called at Chessel House, the Bitterne country seat of David Lance (she wrote in a letter), "we found only Mrs Lance at home and whether she boasts any offspring besides a grand pianoforte did not appear."

It seems the Austens must have known Lance's clergyman brother William, for she adds: "I suppose they must be acting by the orders of Mr Lance of Netherton in this civility, as there seems no other reason for their coming near us. They will not come often, I dare say. They live in a handsome style and are rich, and she seemed to like to be rich, and we gave her to understand that we are far from being so; she will soon feel therefore that we are not worth her acquaintance."

The Austens certainly weren't rich and the long-gone house in Castle Square was rented furnished. It was, according to Jane, a commodious one, with a "pleasant garden bounded on one side

The only known portrait of Jane Austen is by her sister Cassandra.

by the city walls; the top of this wall was sufficiently wide to afford a pleasant walk, with an extensive view, easily accessible to ladies by steps."

When Jane was a resident, Southampton was a beautiful town with elegant buildings and lovely views all around. The family's landlord was the Marquis of Lansdowne who, close by, had incorporated the ruins of the old Southampton castle

A novelist in Castle Square

into a mock-Gothic folly of his own (it was not to last long). A nephew of Jane called it "a fantastic edifice, too large for the space in which it stood, though too small to accord well with its castellated style."

Life seemed to pass pleasantly enough during the family's stay in the then spa town, with its pump room, assembly rooms and baths. Occasionally there was drama, like the fire which broke out at Webbes the pastrycook's, about which Jane wrote vividly.

Walking was always a joy. On at least one visit to the Lances, she wrote, "we went by the ferry and returned by the bridge." Despite Jane's initially rather bitchy reaction to the family at Chessel House, the Austens and the Lances did become friendly. Though on the whole Jane seemed none too interested in the evening entertainments of the town, from time to time she attended a ball at the Dolphin Hotel where she would meet the Lances' two daughters, Mary and Emma.

The novelist seems to have preferred Southampton to Bath. As Maggie Lane, author of *Jane Austen's England* (Robert Hale), has written, it was in her native county and there was the closeness of the sea. But it was the picturesque old town with its walls and towers, the views of the Isle of Wight and the New Forest that must have had the greatest appeal. Writing in 1812, Mary Russell Mitford called it "a lovely spot which combines all that is enchanting in wood and land and water with all that is 'buxom, blythe and debonair' in society.

The Austen's last night in Southampton was Easter Sunday, April 2nd, 1809. They were off on their travels again, this time to a cottage at Chaw-

The mock Gothic castle of the Austens' landlord, the Marquis of Lansdowne.

ton belonging to Jane's brother Edward. For whatever reason, Southampton had not been good for her muse — after she left it her creative powers never deserted her again.

Even in 1808 the family had been thinking of leaving Castle Square. Naval life often made it more convenient for Frank's wife to live elsewhere — the couple had other addresses from time to time at Portsmouth, Yarmouth, Deal and Cowes. The Austens were therefore in need of a smaller home.

It would appear that as a writer Jane Austen could only find satisfaction when living in the country. The garden at Chawton seems to have been a particular delight, though it should not be forgotten that the garden at Castle Square had been a source of pleasure, too. Shortly after their arrival in Southampton she wrote: "We hear that we are envied our house by many people and that the garden is the best in town."

Joe Beckett

Despite winning 31 title fights out of 39 and being the British heavyweight champion for four years until his retirement, Joe Beckett lives on in many elderly memories as the Horizontal Heavyweight, an appellation that is extremely unfair. It's all because of two unfortunate encounters with a debonair Frenchman named Georges Carpentier who later appeared in the movies and in musical comedies.

Joe's story begins in 1893, in Wickham Square. Travelling show people, including the Beckett family, had arrived for the annual fair, and it was there, in his parents' caravan, that the champ-to-be first saw the light. It has been said that Joe was in the ring as early as five. Apocryphal though that statement may be, it's certainly true that he came up the hard way via the time-honoured route of the fairground boxing booths.

When Joe began purses were poor, but he finished his career getting £4,000 a fight and £200 for a music hall appearance. In those days, though not so much now, boxing was considered a branch of showbiz — witness the switch to the film world of prizefighters like Max Baer, "Slapsy" Maxie Rosenbloom and, of course, Joe's nemesis Georges Carpentier.

I remember visiting a friend in Shanklin Road off Hill Lane back in the early Sixties and having Joe, who lived at Number 22, pointed out to me. I had expected a bigger man. Unlike some of today's giants of the ring he was around 5ft 10ins and weighed 13 stone in his heyday — a tough, hard fighter whose left hook was legendary.

1919 was the year when things really happened — in particular the night of February 17 at Holborn Stadium when in five rounds Joe Beckett

Joe in his retirement years.

took the British heavyweight title from Bombardier Billy Wells. Before the 12 months were out, he successfully defended the title against both Frank Goddard and then Dick Smith. But 1919, alas, was also the year of Joe's first unfortunate encounter with Carpentier who knocked him out in one round at Holborn Stadium.

Nevertheless Joe continued to score with other fights. He defended his title again against Roy McCormick, winning a points victory, and in 1923 had a sucessful return match with Dick Smith. The British Empire Heavyweight Championship also came Joe's way when George Cook from Australia was disqualified for holding and the fight was stopped.

Joe's victories, which had included a 1920 win over ex-world heavyweight champion Tommy Burns and another against Pittsburgh dentist Frank Moran (vindication for an earlier defeat), tended to be temporarily forgotten when he again met Carpentier on October 12, 1923, at Olympia. Joe was knocked out in the first round — in 15 to 35 seconds! A fight fan was heard to quip: "I bent down for my programme and missed the fight . . ." It wasn't much of a day for British boxing.

Joe Beckett retired to family life in Southampton, living in Winchester Road before moving to Shanklin Road. Unlike many other successful boxers, he was careful with his money, investing wisely in property. He tried book-making, but gave it up.

Though Joe had his detractors, many people thought the world of him — like the lady who, on his death, wrote to the *Echo* in tribute to "one of the finest and straightest men in the town who would help anyone any time." She revealed that she'd had a husband who was ill-treating her. Her mother sent for Joe, who promptly sorted him out. . . .

What evidently upset some people was Joe's connection with the "black shirt" movement in pre-war days, and it must have been a shock to family and friends when Joe and his wife, publican's daughter Ruth Margaret, were interned under the Defence Regulations in June, 1940 — they were alleged to have been members of the British Union of Fascists.

Richard Thurlow, in his history *Fascism in Britain* (Blackwell) says that the vast majority of interned fascists were British patriots not engaged in subversive or terrorist activities. Evidently the authorities didn't see a lot of point in keeping the Becketts locked up, for they were out before the end of the year. Joe, wrote John Murphy in a 1986 Hampshire Magazine article, had been "sadly misled" politically.

In later years Joe Beckett faded from the headlines, except for domestic items like family weddings and the sad death of his wife in 1952. In 1965, with his death aged 72, he was once again in the news. There were tributes as well as comments about the undefeated champion's supposed "carefulness".

A neighbour spoke of seeing Joe chop up his garden fence for firewood. Another, who described him as "a wonderful man," said she gave him meals and generally looked after him until he had to go into a home. Many people were surprised when he left £32,000 — a tidy sum in 1965.

Joe lies beside his wife at Hollybrook Cemetery, beneath a headstone on which "Peace" is boldly displayed.

Joe's former home in Shanklin Road.

Martin Bell

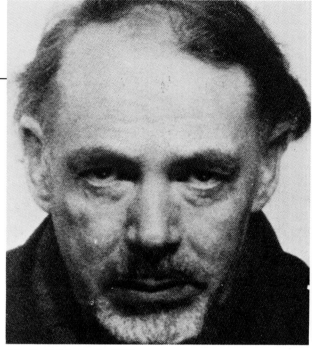

Martin Bell in Leeds, 1975.

Though undeniably a fine Southampton poet, probably its greatest, Martin Bell, in death as in life, is an awkward fellow to fit into any tourist brochure. True, he left his native city as a young man, seldom to return except on visits to his parents, yet Southampton remained in his speaking voice and in his muse. The trouble is that, in the context of civic pride, his voice is caustic and disenchanted.

Posthumously, Bell seems to be achieving the high regard he rarely found outside an admiring circle of fellow bards. He died, like so many other good poets before him, in poverty, having fought a losing battle with alcohol, ill-health and disillusionment.

The man Australian writer Peter Porter has hailed as "one of the major poets writing in English in the second half of the century" was born in Southampton in 1918 and remained there until he was 21.

The son of a railwayman, he won a scholarship to Taunton's School and studied there from 1928 until 1935 before becoming a student at the then University College, now Southampton University, graduating with an English degree in 1938 — he got a diploma in education the following year.

Even then his lack of conformism was marked: the authorities thought him a misfit and suspected him of being the ringleader of a subversive element. In those days, like many another intellectual, Bell was a Communist. One of his lecturers was a leading party member who died in the Spanish Civil War. "He just couldn't keep still at a public meeting," Bell wrote in his valedictory poem *David Guest,* "He would keep turning round and standing up to see who was talking. And this was probably how the bullet got him in the trenches at Jalna".

By conviction Martin Bell was really a conscientious objector; but since the party line forbade that, he volunteered for the Royal Engineers just after the outbreak of war in October, 1939. When he returned he had ceased to be a Communist.

Like so many of his fellow townsmen he was unimpressed with post-war reconstruction and hankered for a pre-blitz Southampton. *High Street, Southampton,* one of his finest poems, makes reference to "neat toy-town blocks of boxes, Noddy shops", and he mourned the street he once knew, when its "shops packed in narrow cliffs rang joy".

The poem makes powerful use of images of both peace and war, from 1918's Armistice Day when "waves of excitement thundered round my pram" to the Thirties when ARMS FOR SPAIN

16

"Shops packed in narrow cliffs rang joy"

boards appeared in the High Street:

"And after Munich put us into heat,
"We went on talking, walking up and down.
"A Saturday addiction, dear Unreal City".

After the blitz Bell returned on leave to find that "nothing was where it was and all was wrong". But the Bargate had "survived as usual, with its air/Of being left over from some other pageant/Waiting to be relieved by Ham the Fifth". His conclusion on the "new" High Street is ironic: "Where is the Phoenix? Surely there was burning."

Southampton buildings making appearances in Bell's work include Sir Edwin Lutyens' Cenotaph which "wedding-caked it above the park, And shadowed birds on Isaac Watts' white shoulders". *Reasons for Refusal* is a sharp but oddly touching account of why Bell would never buy a poppy.

Another is the old Lyric Cinema in St Denys Road, now the premises of PVC Building Supplies, where Bell and his friends "howled and whistled, fidgets on iron seats," watching a musical which inspired one of his rare odes to joy, *To Celebrate Eddie Cantor*.

In London after the war Martin Bell worked as a teacher, married, had a family. A decade later he was one of The Group, a band of poets among whose members were Peter Redgrove, Edward Lucie-Smith, George MacBeth and Peter Porter (who last year edited Bell's *Complete Poems* for Bloodaxe Books).

The year 1964 brought the first real recognition of Bell's stature when he was awarded the first Arts Council poetry bursary. I remember his elderly parents, who lived in Welbeck Avenue, Highfield, coming to the *Southern Evening Echo* office to break their proud news. Three years later came his appointment to Leeds University as Gregory Fellow of Poetry. But by this time, when he was already drinking heavily, his health had begun to decline and in the winter of 1978 he died, having just turned 60.

"Bar Gate survived, as usual, with its air
Of being left over from some other pageant."
—Photo: Southern Newspapers.

Ironically, his first book, *Collected Poems* (Macmillan, 1967) was also his last, though earlier, in 1962, he had shared Volume Three of *Penguin Modern Poets* with the better established George Barker and Charles Causley, certainly this was fitting company for so talented a pen.

Peter Porter, writing in his introduction to the new *Collected Poems*, says his friend's work is less well-known than it deserves to be. His "underground" reputation however, remains high and at long last the wider recognition his work so richly deserves is now being talked about.

Bevis of Hampton

Henry V, so 'tis said, was very fond of the legend of Sir Bevis. It's not surprising, for in its many tellings it remains what used to be dubbed a rattling good yarn. In the knight's far-away romantic world, death and doom were miraculously avoided, heroes were valiant, heroines were pure and swords were magical. The canvas was broad and the piling-up of adventures breathtaking.

Bevis, man or myth, has his name perpetuated in Southampton by a valley, a hill, a street and a couple of pubs. The lions which protected his lady in the story are remembered in the sentinel statues on the Above Bar side of the Bargate, while inside the museum can be seen wooden panels, depicting the knight and his squire Ascupart, which once were displayed on either side of the arch.

The Bevis story was widely known beyond the knight's native town. The French knew him as Beufoes de Hantonne and the Italians called him Buvo De Antona. His exploits were translated into the Scandinavian, Welsh and Slavonic tongues as well as into Italian and French, and *The Romance of Sir Bevois of Hampton* remained a bestseller for centuries.

In just one of the legend's several versions, Bevis was born the son of Sir Guy, Earl of Southampton, around the time of Athelstan and Edgar. The lad's beginnings were unpromising — his mother, having played a part in the murder of his father, has the boy sold to heathen merchants bound for Armenia. There the king takes a fancy to Bevis and appoints him his chamberlain.

As in all tales of this type the king has a comely daughter with whom our hero falls in love. Impressed with his noble deeds, she not only pre-

sents him with a magic sword, Morglay, but an exceedingly bright horse named Arundel. The courtiers become jealous and Bevis is forced to leave.

Many adventures follow, including a seven-year term of imprisonment, but eventually he is able to return to his beloved. Taking the view that discretion is the better part of valour, Bevis disguises himself as an intimate friend of the knight who has sent him in search of the steed Arundel. The queen leads him to the stable, and at the sound of the stranger's voice the horse bursts the seven chains that bind him.

An artist's impression of the oak panels depicting Sir Bevis and Ascapar (Ascupart) at the Bargate Museum.
From a Beric Tempest Colourcard.

A hero from the mists of legend

Bevis vanquishes the giant Ascupart. From Sir Bevis: The Renowned Legend of Southampton, retold and illustrated by Alwyn Sampson *(Shirley Press, 1963).*

Like a ballad heroine receiving the other half of a broken love token, Josian, the king's daughter, thus realises that her lover has come back. Hero, heroine and horse set off for England. En route Bevis leaves Josian in a cave while he sets out to search for food. While he's away two lions come wandering by, but they are so struck by her beauty and obvious virtue that they take up positions on either side of the cave to guard her until the knight's return.

Later the couple are attacked by a giant named Ascupart, but Bevis's enormous strength, and of course his magic sword, vanquishes the enemy. Ascupart becomes his slave and subsequently his squire. One version of the story has the encounter taking place on the shores of Southampton Water,

where Ascupart strikes at Bevis with a massive club. His aim misses and the club lands in the mud.

Ascupart, who is described by one storyteller as 30 feet high with the length of a foot between his eyebrows, sounds and proves a useful ally following our hero's discovery that his rightful inheritance has been usurped by the appositely named Sir Murdour (with whom his mother has been amorously bound). Bevis dispatches the villain in a cauldron of boiling pitch and brimstone . . . some small compensation for those long years of exile . . . and his distraught mother throws herself from the battlements of the Castle.

Even then, the couple still have problems to come. While her lover is away, Josian is forced into marriage by a powerful earl, but the brave lass throttles him in bed. She is condemned to be burnt, but Bevis and Ascupart gallop to the rescue and effect her escape. Bevis and Josian wed, not before time, and go off to pay homage to King Edgar.

No happy ending is yet in sight, for the king's son coverts Arundel. When he tries to steal him, the steed kicks out his brains and Bevis is banished. His return, accompanied now by his two sons, is followed by great slaughter before the king pleads for peace.

One story has it that Bevis and Josian died in each other's arms and that Arundel expired in his stable at the same time. The hero is said to have been buried at the top of Bevois Valley — local spellings include an "o" — and certainly there's a tale of a giant skeleton being dug up when a summer house was being built there in the middle of the 18th Century. Bevis or Ascupart, or just the stuff of another legend?

Philip Brannon

There were too few hours in the day for the likes of Philip Brannon. Dr. A. T. Markwick, researching his life, found him described in the street directories of his day as an artist, printer, stationer, architect, engineer, professor of watercolour painting and decorative design, and house and estate agent. His time was that period of intense creativity and inventiveness, the mid-19th Century. Brannon, born in 1817, was in many ways the personification of the industrious Victorian age.

To his many accomplishments could be added another: inventor. The man now known mainly for his sometimes rather over-imaginative but charming engravings of Southampton scenes drew up plans for navigable "balloon ships" (even though, as Southern Daily Echo editor C. F. Carr wrote in 1940, his "air theories could scarcely have been expected to stand up to practical tests"). He also took out patents for, among many other things, the fireproofing of buildings, road surfacing and reinforced concrete.

In practical terms, though, Brannon never really made it. He was in and out of the bankruptcy courts and died in poverty. But his beginnings were full of promise.

Born at Wootton in the Isle of Wight, third son of George Brannon, engraver, printer and publisher, Philip was a young man of ideals as well as ideas, and in his early years started a "ragged school" for boys, and later girls as well, at Newport. "Leave the world the better for your having lived in it" was Brannon's motto, and he continued to espouse good causes in a practical way throughout his busy and eventful life.

He moved away from the Island to make his

Philip Brannon's trade card, showing his shop front and incorporating other Southampton views.

home in Southampton around 1844, setting up as an engraver and art master. One of his sidelines was the designing of trade cards — many local tradesmen were his clients. Seen today, these cards provide intriguing glimpses of long vanished aspects of the town.

His guides, including one of Southampton (1850), with their exquisitely engraved steelplate ilustrations, enjoyed a wide readership then and are highly valued collector's items today. The engravings, with their leafy trees and stovepipe-hatted and crinolined passers-by, have a delightful flavour all their own.

Though the Echo's "Townsman" ("Mike" Mitchell), writing during the Thirties in his Occasional Notes, praises Brannon for his detail, he refers to the artistic licence he allows himself in the way of perspective and in the suggested "extent and luxuriance" of his vegetation.

The story is told that when Brannon was instructing his poor Newport boys in drawing there was one boy in particular who took delight

Engraver, architect and inventor

Philip Brannon.

in upsetting the class. No Squeers or Murdstone, the teacher wasn't going to put up with that sort of behaviour and promptly swung the miscreant by the scruff of the neck and over the heads of his fellows to the front of the class. He was studious from that time on!

Years later, when the Unitarian Church of the Saviour in London Road, Southampton, was being built — Brannon was the architect — a young stonecarver working on the project confessed to his former teacher: 'I'm the boy you conquered in the school at Newport, sir, and that night I made up my mind to be a stonecarver."

Brannon was brought up as a Unitarian and married the first of his two wives at the Unitarian Church in Newport in 1844. It is sad, though, that the Southampton church he designed, the foundation stone of which was laid on July 30, 1859, should no longer exist as a testament to his skills and faith: it was destroyed by enemy action in the Second World War.

Brannon's patent "intensiphone", one of his many acoustic inventions, was partly embodied in a canopy soundboard at the Church of the Saviour, and in 1860 he gave a demonstration in Southampton of an apparatus he had thought up for amplifying the voice of a speaker — he afterwards complained that it had been pirated.

Not long after he had won a commission to design the now truncated East Park memorial to five-times-mayor Richard Andrews — the wheelwright's son they called Southampton's Dick Whittington — but had lost out on a design for the Hartley Institution (forerunner of the University), Brannon returned to his native Isle of Wight.

By 1863 he had become Clerk and Surveyor to Shanklin's Local Board of Health and later still Inspector of Nuisances. Though he continued with his illustrations and his painting, he was in the bankruptcy courts several times. The Seventies found him in London, drumming up interest in his flying machines and in all manner of other engineering ideas. Finally, once again on the verge of financial disaster, Brannon died at his London office in 1890.

An unsuccessful man, yes. But a memorable and remarkable one? Yes again. Happily, his prints are still widely admired, and down at Seaton in Devon his bridge over the Axe stands as a lasting tribute to his engineering ability.

Frederick Lee Bridell

The man they called Southampton's greatest painter — known to his fellow townsfolk as genial if impulsive but utterly dedicated to his art — was born in a hovel in downtown Houndwell, son of a poor carpenter who wanted his son to be a chip off the old block. But at 15, when he became a 15-shillings-a-week housepainter's lad, Frederick Lee Bridell had already developed an astonishing aptitude for sketching.

He sold his first drawings for half a crown, yet by the time he was 21 he'd exhibited at the Royal Academy. After his death his works realised £1,000 each, and more.

Bridell was born at Houndwell Place, near the present site of Debenham's store, in 1830. His humble beginnings — the youngster began his working life as a pageboy — could have stymied his ascent in life, but his early art work was so remarkable that people soon began talking about the amazing teenager.

His portrait of friend Henry Rose, painted when Bridell was 18, was seen by a dealer, who promptly gave him a five-year contract to copy Old Masters — a task which taught him a great deal. Two years after exhibiting at the RA, when he was 21, the young artist travelled abroad to Paris and Munich, a trip from which his love affair with the Alps derived.

Home again by 1858, he had acquired a patron, James Woolf, and was living far from lowly Houndwell at Highfield Lodge, where he painted *The Temple of Love* — a work inspired by Spenser's *Faerie Queene*. A contemporary critic dubbed it "Turnerian" . . . and he wasn't the last authority to note the influence of Turner's light effects. Reminders of Poussin, the Dutch school and contempor-

Bridell's 1848 portrait of his friend Henry Rose.

ary German Romantics were also noted in Bridell's work.

Another summer visit to Europe was the curtain raiser to his giant masterpiece *The Colosseum at Rome by Midnight,* a 7ft 6in by 5ft work typical of the Olympian style of mid-Victorian painting which later had an equivalent in the films of Cecil B. de Mille and other Hollywood directors.

Because of its subtleties in the conveying of mists and shadows, few reproductions can do jus-

Southampton's Greatest Artist

tice to this painting — now in Southampton Art Gallery, though it's only there by a sheer fluke. After a 1913-14 exhibition at Nottingham, it vanished and didn't surface until 16 years later when someone spotted it at a London hotel. "The Colosseum" was sold to an enthusiast the very next day!

Let Frederick Bridell describe the painting for himself:

"The scattered sculpture in the foreground is part of a temple supposed to be dedicated to Venus and Rome, and the Capucian monks burying their dead is typical of modern Rome whose worthlessness and decay we see daily, contrasting with the old Rome typified by the grand old ruins whose entire decay has not yet come."

The Coliseum (as we would spell it today) was begun by Vespasian and dedicated to Titus in AD80, at which festival 5,000 wild beasts were slaughtered in the arena.

Modern Rome, as Bridell found it, was still a violent place, and when the tubercular artist braved the midnight mists of a malarial district to paint his masterpiece — the moon had to be at just the right height, he said later — he took a couple of thugs with him as bodyguards.

The painting's history was chequered, to say the least. Exhibited at the Academy the year it was painted, it went under Christie's hammer in 1864 when it realised £500. Subsequently it was sold for a much higher sum.

The man who spotted it in London, years after its disappearance, was Southampton businessman and eccentric William Burrough Hill. After 1900 Hill amassed a large quantity of the prolific painter's work and even named his Millbrook home Bridell Lodge. . . .

The career of the talented working-class painter proved tragically short. Even at the time of the misty midnight work on "the Colosseum" he was ailing, but according to his wife and fellow artist Eliza Fox, whom he married a year before his death at 33, he went on producing canvas after canvas to within six months of his final illness.

He left behind a remarkable body of work: oils, watercolours, drawings. The Art Gallery of his native city proudly owns about 40 subjects. Local ones include *A View of Southampton* in oils, a watercolour (*Eaglehurst from Calshot Point*) and a pencil sketch of a windmill near Hythe.

But even in the artist's day Southampton had pride in Bridell. His patron Wolff had a roomful of paintings at Bevois Mount House. Its name: the Bridell Gallery.

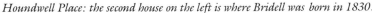

Houndwell Place: the second house on the left is where Bridell was born in 1830.

C. F. Carr

C. F. Carr: the dynamo at the dictaphone.

Clarence Firbank Carr, the most dynamic editor in the Southern Echo's hundred-year history, found the world an endlessly fascinating place. He scooped up interests like a starving man, zooming in on pond life, local history, archaeology and countless other subjects with equal hunger. He wrote books on journalism, gliding, beekeeping. He wrote poetry, plays and scripts for silent films. And all this in the little spare time he had as a busy newspaperman.

"C.F.C.", as he was known to generations of Echo people, was born a Victorian — on June 15, 1892 — and embodied the qualities of that century's amazing cast of polymaths. The son of a Coast Guard, who raised the Southbourne station's flag to announce his arrival, he was brought up in Morvah, Cornwall, and later at Preston, Weymouth, from where he travelled daily by train to Dorchester for his first job as a cub reporter on the Dorset County Chronicle.

The 14-year-old avid reader and self-taught shorthand writer watched a gamekeeper being sentenced to death for killing a girl, an incident which upset him for a fortnight. He also found himself distastefully viewing dead bodies at inquests and, while on the obituary trail, in private homes. It was a hard school and his brief was wide: he learnt book-keeping, the hand-setting of type and even advertisement canvassing.

One evening a man he afterwards discovered was the great Thomas Hardy called at the office and proffered some fatherly advice — later C.F.C. rented the cottage where the novelist was born and, as the author of a screenplay for the silent film company, Hepworth, was to approach Hardy with a scenario for *Far from the Madding Crowd*.

The film was never made.

After war service in the Middle East and a spell on an evening paper in Newport, Mon., he plunged into another battlefield — the circulation war between the Weymouth-based Dorset Daily Echo and the Dorset Daily Press which were both started in the same week. Though Clarence Carr was offered jobs on both, he chose the Echo. After three years "fighting like mad for exclusives", it won the battle and took the Daily Press over. In 1921 he became the Dorset Echo's editor.

The General Strike of 1926 gave C.F.C an opportunity which led to the modernisation of all three Echos (Southampton, Bournemouth and Weymouth). It happened like this. Two years before, Clarence had been promoted assistant editor of the flagship paper at Southampton but, with the strike imminent, was ordered to return to Weymouth. Given a free hand to get the Echo out with a depleted staff, he seized the chance to produce not only a paper with a smaller, more manageable format but one with headlined stories rather than advertisements on the front page. The new design proved so popular that it was afterwards introduced at the sister papers, too.

Clarence proved himself the sub-editors'

The man who invented "Soton" and "Sotonian"

friend when, back at Above Bar, he introduced the abbreviations "Soton" and "Sotonian", a boon for headline writers struggling with the unwieldy Southampton and, even worse, Southamptonian. While nobody ever refers to "Soton", the other word remains in regular conversational use — who hasn't heard someone say "I'm a Sotonian"?

After the Dorset circulation wars and the General Strike the Thirties were fairly uneventful for C.F.C. He did meet up a couple of times, though, with Lawrence of Arabia (whom he had seen enter Damascus in triumph during the Great War), and his play about Charles Dickens, written with local historian "Mike" Mitchell ("Townsman"), was put on at the Grand Theatre.

The Second World War brought more drama. After his company's offices at Southampton and Weymouth were destroyed in 1941, the year he became editor of the Southern Echo, C.F.C. took on the production at Bournemouth of the three Echos, motoring down daily for three years. And as general manager and editor-in-chief of Southern Newspapers Ltd (1948-57) he saw the grand opening by Earl Mountbatten of the new post-war

The long-vanished Grand Theatre, where the Carr-Mitchell play on Dickens was put on before the war, is seen here in the late Forties, as yet not reopened following its war damage.
—Photo: Southern Newspapers.

Above Bar premises in 1955.

He didn't welcome his retirement when it came in 1957, but it turned out to be a long one. "The born journalist" (his first editor's description) just carried on writing, turning out a vast number of articles for a wide variety of publications — most notably The Scotsman. He also kept on talking.

The raconteur who once co-wrote a book on public speaking liked to tell how he nearly got into trouble with the police outside the old Savage Club in Carlton Terrace. As a member he had long wanted to confirm that a statue outside the club was by the sculptor Matthew Noble, a kinsman on his mother's side. He began climbing it to see if he could discover if there was an inscription attributing the work to Noble when suddenly there came a "nah then, what's all this?" from a passing copper.

C.F.C. managed to convince the constable of his intention — the Pc even gave him a leg up! And, yes, the statue WAS a Matthew Noble. More obscurely, Clarence Firbank Carr was related to the novelist Ronald Firbank. C.F.C. disliked the name Clarence but liked Firbank — he wrote his poetry under the pen name Charles Firbank.

He died in November, 1979, at 87, leaving a widow, Sybil (now dead) and two sons, John, who followed his father into journalism and is now in public relations, and Michael, an insurance executive. Though, oddly, unmentioned in the centenary supplement of the Echo he once edited, it's true to say that this remarkable man had a powerful impact both on his paper and on local affairs. Nationally, too, for it was through his initiative that the Guild of British Newspaper Editors was set up.

25

William Cantelo

The inventor of the Cantelo capstan, still in use for much of this century, was a Southampton man from a family of Isle of Wight gunsmiths, and it was William Cantelo's own gun connection that made him the focal point of a strange Victorian mystery.

He was one of those industrious types who typified the bustling 19th Century. Forever bristling with ideas, he certainly diversified his interests. Not only did he run a Northam engineering yard employing 40 people. He was also a shopkeeper in French Street, a publican (the Old Tower Inn in Bargate Street) and a musician (bandmaster of the 2nd Hampshires).

He held his band practices in Arundel Tower. It was in the tower, behind locked doors, that he busied himself with his inventions. Use of an underground passage assisted the secrecy.

Residents in nearby, long-gone cottages would hear gunfire coming from the direction of the tower, and it soon transpired that busy Mr Cantelo was engaged in creating a quick-firing machine gun. Soon all Southampton was talking about the gun.

One day he told his family that it was finished and that he was off for an extended holiday. They all agreed he needed one and had earned it. So William kissed his pretty wife (known as "the Belle of Newport" in their courting days), embraced his three children, packed up his gun . . . and disappeared.

Since Cantelo had said he would be away for three months, no mystery surrounded him at first — he had left home for long periods before, purportedly visiting the Continent on business. Eventually, of course, the family became anxious — and they were particularly dismayed to discover that the head of the household had taken a large sum of money with him.

None of them ever saw him again, though his two sons were convinced they spotted him years later at Waterloo Station. As time went by several attempts were made to locate the inventor: one trail led to America but died away to nothing.

Then came the news that an American had perfected a quick-firing machine gun in London, but was offering it to the American Government . . . though in the end the British bought it.

The Cantelos took one look at a photograph of the inventor, Hiram Maxim from Maine, and were convinced that he was "Father". And in any case the gun sounded just like the Cantelo invention to them.

William Cantelo.

26

Was he really Hiram Maxim?

Hiram Maxim.

So the two sons set out to find Maxim. One day they spotted him about to board a train at Waterloo. "Father!", they shouted. Hiram looked round, smiled, and asked them what they wanted. But then the train started to move before they could get a reaction to their answer: "Come and visit Mother."

Though Maxim had a strong American accent, the young men were sure he was really William Cantelo. They were just as convinced when they saw him a second time before he left their lives forever. They went down to Maxim's home in Bexley, Kent, but saw him drive off by the rear entrance. By co-incidence or design?

The Cantelos weren't the only ones to believe that the two inventors were one and the same. An old neighbour spotted a man he thought was Cantelo at an Essex artillery display. "Mr Cantelo!" he cried out, and the man who was Maxim turned round instantly.

"Townsman" (E. A. Mitchell) of the pre-war *Echo,* who was always intrigued by this supposed case of mistaken identity, recalled another Sotonian addressing Maxim as Cantelo in London and being threatened with the law. By this time, perhaps, the American was becoming fed up with the whole business.

Another coincidence, though, provides spice to a strange tale. Cantelo, it seems, was fond of quoting maxims; he carried a book of them in his pocket and even referred to his invention as "my maxim gun!"

A word about this man Maxim (1840-1916). He came to England in 1881, was naturalised in 1900 and knighted in 1901. The "Maxim" was the first fully automatic machine gun and it made his fortune, though he had other modest inventions to his name — including a mousetrap! His son Hiram Junior's biographical study *A Genius in the Family* was filmed in 1946 with Don Ameche as Maxim.

But whatever happened to William Cantelo?

The wedding of Mr and Mrs Hiram Maxim (Don Ameche and Myrna Loy) in the 1946 Hollywood "biopic" A Genius in the Family. Photo: Universal.

Comte de Cartrie

The Comte de Cartrie.

There was something a little out of the ordinary about the French labourer who in 1796 sought and found employment with retired surgeon James Dott at Bitterne Grove, an attractive country house with a fine view of the river Itchen. Yet someone who knew the man at Bitterne could write that he lacked the polish of the Court — "his misfortunes had brought him to think himself on a level with the most humble with whom he might converse."

Certainly French Revolution refugee Toussaint-Ambroise Talour de la Cartrie de la Villeniere, usually called Comte de Cartrie, had suffered greatly before he came to Bitterne. He had distinguished himself in the abortive Royalist revolt at La Vendee and later became involved in a series of adventures which might have come from the pages of The Scarlet Pimpernel. He was forced to adopt disguises, he moved stealthily by night and he slept in the hollows of trees.

Eventually he managed to get to England, where he offered his services to the Prince de Leon, commander of a body of French Royalist soldiers who were awaiting the 19th Century equivalent of a Bay of Pigs venture — an attack on the Brittany coast. The Count joined the expedition in Jersey; but, like the Vendee revolt in which he had fought earlier, the escapade was doomed. Stormy weather and treachery in the ranks of the invaders contributed to the failure.

According to his memoirs, the Count was "more dead than alive" when he returned to Jersey in December, 1795 — a man of 53, it should be remembered, was elderly in those days. The merchants there helped him out with a supply of clothes and, through the good offices of the Prince

de Bouillon, an ex-British Navy officer who lived at the island's Castle de Montorgueil, he was given a shilling a day for a servant.

After a month he found one, but assured the fellow that he couldn't afford him. The man said he wanted nothing and even loaned the Count three guineas to repay the merchants for the clothes they supplied. The "servant" then gained employment elsewhere but insisted on joining the Count when the French were ordered to leave Jersey for Southampton in July.

After all his privations and misfortunes beneath the shadow of the guillotine, the Count deserved a break. Imagine how he must have felt, then, on being informed that his services to the Royalist forces were no longer required. He was in debt, he had no prospect of employment and, on top of all that, his "servant" demanded the return of his three guineas.

De Cartrie, in his memoirs, tells of the man visiting him at Romsey "where many French were established". There the "servant" came up with a means whereby the debt could be repaid. It seems the man had obtained employment as a gardener in Southampton; he asssured the Count that he could get a similar job for him at the same place.

So, the memoirs continue, "I put the little clothes I had into my portmanteau, and throwing it on my shoulder I followed my domestic, or more properly speaking, my master, as by him I was now governed, and for him I was now going

Refugee aristocrat who worked as a gardener

to hard labour to satisfy his demand on me." Life had certainly been different at the old family chateau near Angers!

On August 3, 1796, the man presented the Count to Mr. Dott at Bitterne Grove as a labourer seeking work and he was at once accepted. The Count goes on: "I continued then to work for ten hours each day till the month of December, when having gained enough to settle with my servant we both left our work, for immediately on his payment he set off for London."

De Cartrie, who had taken a small lodging nearby, was then confined to his cottage by a violent attack of gout. Fortunately it wasn't long before his "state of distress and abject poverty" was discovered by gentlemen of the neighbourhood, without whose aid he might have died.

In April, 1797, the Count moved to another lodging, at Itchen Ferry. The government allowed him a shilling a day and an additional shilling for a servant, though he thought it prudent not to employ one. The gentry continued to be kind, providing him with victuals and, in due course, a house to live in free of charge.

Things were looking up, and the month of July, 1798, brought the happy news that, on the death of the rapacious Robespierre, his wife and

family had been included in the Act of Amnesty which permitted them to take possession of their chateau. The Count managed to raise £50 to begin his journey home, and there the autobiography of one of Southampton's most interesting visitors comes to an end.

The Count's memoirs were composed during his Southampton years and translated by a local man whose identity remains unknown — could it have been Jane Austen's friend David Lance, of Chessel House, who gave his name to Lances Hill? Anyway, the bound translation turned up at a Torquay bookshop in 1904 and was published by John Lane (the Bodley Head) a couple of years later.

De Cartrie appears to have been a most pleasant man, generous within his means, mild-mannered, kindly and popular with his fishermen neighbours, even though they didn't care for the French: neither, it appears, did the Count, who — according to the translator — found them quarrelsome and avoided their company.

The Count returned home in 1800, but what happened to him after that? We learn that this stout defender of "the Throne and the Altar" continued to lead an impoverished life and, at 81, as one of many post-Restoration petitioners, had his application for a pension turned down.

Nothing was heard from the Count de Cartrie after 1824. Bitterne Grove, where he had toiled, passed into several hands and for most of this century has been the home of the Brothers of Christian Instruction who administer St. Mary's College. The French connection continues, for their teaching order was at one time in refuge here from French anti-clericalism.

Bitterne Grove today, home of the brothers of St. Mary's College.
Photo: Southern Newspapers.

Sir Christopher Cockerell

The inventor of the sidewall and amphibious hovercraft revealed his interest in engineering at an early age — he harnessed his mother's sewing machine to his steam engine when he was ten and made his school's wireless when he was 13! Thirty years later he set himself a problem: how to make a boat go faster. Little step by little step, it led to the hovercraft concept.

Sir Christopher, as he became in 1969, was born on June 4, 1910, the son of Sir Sydney Cockerell, who was secretary to William Morris and the Kelmscott Press from 1892 to 1898 and director of the Fitzwilliam Museum, Cambridge, from 1908 to 1937 (Sir Sydney, to his son's delight, was portrayed by Sir John Gielgud in *The Best of Friends* at London's Apollo Theatre in 1988).

From 1935 until 1951 Sir Christopher led the Marconi team responsible for the design of the navigational and communication equipment fitted to our bombers during the war and, later, other equipment which automatically scanned the frequencies of the German coastal radio stations — recording the signals from them in such a way that their positions could be pinpointed and then bombed out of existence before D-Day.

The Fifties saw a change of direction for Sir Christopher and his wife Margaret — they bought a caravan business on the Norfolk Broads which in turn led to another enterprise, boat-hiring. It was during those happy boating years that Christopher Cockerell conceived the idea of the hovercraft.

In October, 1956, in the basement of his patent agent's office, he demonstrated to members of the technical departments of the Admiralty and the RAF his newest and most unusual craft: a tiny oval-shaped balsa model, equipped with a motor, which whizzed around the room supported on a self-generated cushion of air. This, of course, was the first demonstration of a hovercraft, fruit of years of thought and experimentation. Up to this stage, Sir Christopher told me, the project was fun, but from then on it was exhausting, disappointing and frustrating . . . because it was necessary to convince the sceptics that it worked, and to try to raise the necessary money.

The project was classified for three months, which meant that the inventor couldn't talk to anyone about it unless that person was cleared, and Ministries weren't prepared to spend the money to clear anybody. Saunders-Roe produced a favourable report on the project, but at a meeting attended by the armed services representatives it was decided to do nothing: nor could Cockerell get the project declassified.

But then a Swiss engineer who had visited Saunders-Roe told the Swiss press about it, and it was this leak which finally declassified the hovercraft. Now its inventor was free to go to the National Research Development Corporation, which finally backed the project. In October, 1958, a Saunders-Roe design team began work on the first experimental hovercraft, and in July of the following year it made a successful crossing of the

The SR-NI hovercraft which made a successful debut crossing of the Channel in 1959.

"Is it a ship? Is it a plane?"

Sir Christopher Cockerell.

Channel to commemorate Bleriot's historic flight 50 years earlier.

The NRDC formed Hovercraft Development Ltd., which got together a small research team (a big project on a shoestring), and a little later Saunders-Roe, now Westland, created the British Hovercraft Corporation. Looking back, Sir Christopher told me: "Two top executives of NRDC accepted seats on the board of the BHC, thus making it very difficult for other companies to get fair treatment. I therefore had to tell the Press about it, and of course they were furious with me — they both separately sent me a letter sacking me, which was rather amusing."

The upshot was that Vosper's got their licence and Hovermarine a small amount of financial help. Sir Christopher had, in fact, sacrificed his job for the good of his invention.

During a Southampton Junior Chamber of Commerce address in 1976 the inventor told of being asked to take his invention to the USA, adding that if he'd had any sense he'd have done so but felt he ought to try to make a contribution to his own country. One of his early ideas put up to Saunders-Roe was the use of skirts. "They would have none of it," says Sir Christopher (later a member of Hovercraft Development Ltd., Denys Bliss, invented the segmented skirt which Westland eventually adopted).

According to Sir Christopher, hovercraft remains less than half developed, though its inventor has gained world recognition and many awards, the greatest of which came in 1969 when, already a CBE, he received a knighthood in the New Year Honours. In 1971, 18 years after starting work on the hovercraft, and after carrying all the expenses of the first six years, he finally received a cheque for £150,000.

Hovercraft have carried 34 million people and millions of cars across the Channel — in a faster time, points out Sir Christopher, than will be achieved after billions of pounds have been spent on "the Victorian idea" of a Channel tunnel! Sooner or later, he believes, hovercraft development will be taken further. It is, he reminds us, the only vehicle which can make full use of an atomic power plant, thus gaining a greater speed than that of ships — plus unlimited range.

In 1985 Sir Christopher, once a resident of Ardnave Crescent, Bassett, but now living outside Southampton at Hythe, celebrated his 75th birthday. Still the visionary, he chose the occasion to speak to the local press of a solar-powered future ("the sun produces 1,000 times as much energy as we need"). Energy storage still occupied the mind of a man who had also designed the Cockerell Raft, a device to harness wave power. Though cutbacks scotched that programme, the Government went on to honour Sir Christopher in a less practical way — early in 1988 they named an Antarctic penisula after him and he was also made an RDI (Royal Designer for Industry).

Herbert Collins

The most important achitect in the housing field that Southampton has ever seen—that was how former City Architect Leon Berger described Herbert Collins. Anyone who has walked down Uplands Way in Highfield, preferably on a sunny summer afternoon, will be aware of architectural beauty of a distinctive, quietly elegant and unostentatiously harmonious kind.

That Herbert Collins was, as a young man, associated with the Garden City movement comes as no surprise. So was his brother William, who founded the Rookfield Garden Village Company at Muswell Hill, where their father had been a speculative "Metroland" builder. After William Collins Senior moved to Southampton in 1911, Herbert dreamed of turning Marchwood into a garden city.

Nothing came of the scheme, despite the financial support of his father and the encouragement of the movement's founder Sir Ebenezer Howard, who had earlier welcomed Herbert to the board of directors at Welwyn Garden City. According to his biographer, Robert Williams, Herbert Collins remained committed to the ideal of a garden city in that spot for the rest of a long and rewarding life.

People familiar with Welwyn GC will find echoes of it in the Uplands Estate at Highfield, Southampton, the architect's first, and the pattern-maker for what followed. The style is "Georgian-cottage", with charming use made of grass borders, trees and open spaces. There is nothing quite like a Collins estate—others flowered at Bassett Green, Coxford, Thornhill (I was born in a Collins house in Thornhill Park Road).

There were many interesting projects, and not

Uplands Way: the jewel in the Collins architectural crown.

only in Southampton, to fill a career spanning 66 years. They ranged from designs for his father's Muswell Hill estate in 1906 to extensions to his Brookvale Road, Highfield, home in the Seventies—three years before his death at 90.

The people who founded the Garden City movement in the century's early years were idealists—people like Bernard Shaw were among the supporters—and, indeed, idealism dominated Herbert Collins's entire life. He wasn't just concerned with designing attractive houses but with the people who lived in them and with people everywhere.

He founded the local branch of the League of Nations Union in 1924, building it up into one of the most successful in the country; and after the Second World War he was for 24 years secretary of the United Nations Association Southampton branch, establishing an international charities shop for world peace, a schools' public speaking competition on that subject, and the annual UN flag-raising at the Civic Centre on United Nations Day.

He dreamed of a garden city

Herbert Collins.

The Collins memorial gate.

He was a pioneer of the Local Civic Trust, now the City of Southampton Society, helped to found the Hampshire branch of the Council for the Preservation of Rural England, and was busy in many other good causes. Though a man of private means which allowed him to work as he wanted without relying on commissions, Herbert Collins was Liberal with Labour leanings and was an advocate of land nationalisation.

Certainly it's true to say that he did not always find favour with the architectural establishment. Much of his housing work was set up by the Collins family, and often by the architect himself against the RIBA code of conduct forbidding the financial involvement of architects in building developments.

Could this be why, when he died in 1975, none of the architectural and planning journals gave him an obituary? It wasn't always thus, for time was when the same journals acclaimed him. In the Twenties and Thirties his work was illustrated in national architectural journals and in the major European publications.

Southampton, though, did not forget him. A Highfield memorial gate, following an appeal by the City of Southampton Society, was opened by his daughter, Mrs. Julie Ozwell, in 1987.

Herbert Collins was a man of great height whose reserved manner was often mistaken for aloofness. Shy, modest and diffident rather than austere, he was always dignified, even on that curious post-war occasion when some disgruntled person placed a redundant Corporation tram on a plot opposite his Highfield home. He was, too, generous by stealth to those in need, as befitted a true idealist.

N. J. Crisp

In the mid-Fifties ex-RAF man Norman Crisp was into his thirties and only just getting down to a long-standing ambition to write. One summer's morning he woke up determined to conquer his inertia and do something about it. He said to himself: "If I don't start now I'll still be going to do it when I'm 60."

So write he did, and it was a decision that has paid off handsomely down the years. When he first began writing — short stories for the magazine market — he was working as Southampton area manager for a pest control firm by day and turning out 500 words by night. He had a modest success, too: his stories were published on both sides of the Atlantic — three were sold to America for £2,000, and some were broadcast on the BBC.

It was the BBC which gave him his first break in television with a thriller called *People of the Night*. This was in 1959 when its author was manager of Streamline, the Southampton taxi fleet, an experience which must have helped in giving authenticity to the play's setting — the office of a provincial radio taxi firm. The drama was so successful that another was commissioned and N. J. Crisp's career took off from there.

The next few years saw him established as one of the best craftsmen in the business, and it was not really a surprise when, a decade later, he received the Writiers' Guild of Great Britain award as the Best Writer of British TV series for

N. J. Crisp.

his contributions to *Dixon of Dock Green, Dr. Finlay's Casebook* and *The Revenue Men*. He had been runner-up two years previously.

He went on to write scripts for *The Expert,* a series he co-devised (starring Marius Goring as a forensic scientist), *The Brothers, Colditz, The Secret Army.* . . . And, as with his first TV play, he often drew on his own experiences for the yarns he spun. His wartime service with the RAF had included a spell with the Glider Pilot Regiment which helped him later when he came to write *Colditz,* and an episode of *The Expert* showed the problems of a boy suffering from a condition that first plagued Norman Crisp in 1954 — tunnel vision.

It foreshadowed a more serious condition which left him blind in one eye, affected the sight in the other and slowed up his work considerably. Now registered blind, he reads his scripts with a magnifier. He has had other health problems too — operations on the spinal cord 16 years ago and another in 1988 for the removal of a kidney.

But despite the setbacks the Southampton-born Old Tauntonian has kept busy, turning out not only TV series and short stories but West End plays and a batch of novels. Fortunately, he has always had a supportive family: his wife Marguerite — known as Rita — is his guide, and his children, three sons and a daughter, act as his researchers.

One of his daughters-in-law, a doctor, helped him with his play *Fighting Chance* which was such a hit at the Shaftesbury Theatre. And, of course, his own experiences have always proved helpful, as with his 1983 novel *Yesterday's Gone* for which he drew upon memories of his wartime pilot training.

Norman Crisp, by a combination of hard work and talent, has been able to fulfil his early ambition to earn a living from writing and is forever hopeful that his next work will be his best work. The compulsion has obviously helped him triumph over

The Abbotts Way home of N. J. Crisp.

adversity, for he continues to be prolific — 1988 saw a novel, *In the Long Run,* coming out during the run of another successful West End play, *Dangerous Obsession.*

Years ago, not long after moving to Abbott's Way, Highfield, he wrote in an attic room at his spacious home, though the requirements of TV team production meant that he had to spend quite a lot of time in London. These days he writes in London and relaxes at Highfield. The location of the writing process — "sheer hard work," he once admitted — is probably irrelevant. What matters is getting down to it. It was an auspicious day back in the Fifties when he decided to do just that. . . .

The Rev. Harold Davidson

The story of Sholing-born Harold Davidson never fails to raise a smile. In the far-off Depression days of the early Thirties it was considered positively bracing, a dirty vicar tale guaranteed to take unemployment and the rise of fascism off the front pages and from the minds of the people for a diverting while. Yet his story is essentially tragic. Scandal always is.

Just think of it. A supposed moral crusader, defrocked for immoral behaviour with teenage tarts, returns to his first profession, show business, and ends his life as a latter-day failed Daniel, fatally mauled by a lion at a Skegness funfair. No wonder the Rector of Stiffkey — even this Norfolk place name appears appropriately ridiculous — inspired both broadcasters and composers (he was the hero of two flop musicals in 1969).

Harold Davidson was born in Sholing, son of the Vicar, on July 14, 1875. His father, the Rev. Francis Davidson, had come to the parish some nine years previously and, according to his son's biographer Tom Cullen (in *The Prostitutes' Padre*, published by The Bodley Head in 1975), preached there to a half-empty church every Sunday for 48 years.

The vicar, a tiny man with a huge beard who rode round the parish on a tricycle, evidently had an uphill struggle leading his flock along the paths of righteousness. Sometimes (according to a later Vicar, the Rev. Harry Marsh) drunken husbands, with whom the Rev. Francis Davidson had remonstrated, threatened to throw him into Miller's Pond, but the Vicar remained unintimidated.

It was a tough parish in those days, with what were then called the genteel outnumbered by dock worker families and a strong Gypsy element. The

The Rector of Stiffkey.

Vicar impressed everyone with his practical Christianity. Parishioners noted that he never turned anyone from his door and was generous to vagrants.

This being Victorian Britain, social distances were kept and little Harold, who at six went to join the sons of Merchant Navy officers at Banister Court School over the river in central Southampton, wasn't allowed to play with the sons of stevedores or Romanies. At 15 he changed schools, moving to Croydon where his maiden aunts lived.

Much to the chagrin of the Vicar of Sholing, Harold took up the stage rather the cloth, becom-

Defrocked clergyman fatally mauled by a lion

ing a professional reciter working the masonic lodges and the mechanics' institutes. This career was not to last long. Having dissuaded a 16-year-old girl from jumping into the Thames and thus stumbling upon his vocation, he became the 28th member of his family to follow holy orders.

It took Harold five years to get a degree, working his way through Oxford by undertaking theatre work. So great was his love of the stage that, six months after becoming Rector of Stiffkey in May, 1906, he married an Irish actress, Molly Saurin. He was to haunt stage doors as a chaplain to the Actors' Church Union and even embarked, in 1908, on an ill-fated theatrical adventure.

This was a revival of a musical named *Dorothy*, financed in partnership with his old school friend from Banister Court, Maundy Gregory (another vicar's son whose equally scandalous story is told elsewhere in this book). "I am ruined!," cried Davidson — not for the last time.

What with hanging about stage doors and devoting a great deal of time in London saving nubile nymphs from a fate worse than death, it isn't surprising that the Rector neglected his parish as well as his family (his wife's last child wasn't his). Indeed, his spending all week in the

Sholing Parish Church.

metropolis and only getting back in time for Sunday services was bound to make him enemies. He found a formidable one in churchwarden Major Philip Hamond.

Lack of punctuality was something he had inherited with his father and the Major didn't like to see it in a parson — sometimes Davidson was so late for a Sunday service that he found the congregation had gone home. Even more upsetting for Major Hamond were rumours that the village labourers were enjoying the favours of youthful prostitutes invited by the Rector to spend a morally uplifting weekend at the Rectory.

When Harold Davidson was charged in 1932 with immorality under the Clergy Discipline Act of 1892, the court was told that he had taken a girl to Paris to find her a job. This was nothing new. Earlier, as a theatrical chaplain, he escorted Folies Bergere recruits to France, stopping off at his father's Sholing vicarage where, according to his sister, some of the dancers joined the Girls' Friendly Society.

Though he was found guilty and later defrocked, it's fair to say that of 40 females interviewed only one declared that the Rector had behaved immorally. But it was the evidence of this girl, plus a suspicious Press photo (taken with Davidson's unwise permission), that sealed his fate — many of his parishioners believed him guilty of nothing more than an obsession with helping pretty girls in moral danger.

This extraordinary story had an even more bizarre end, with Davidson exhibiting himself in a barrel on Blackpool's Golden Mile before his final mauling at Skegness Amusement Park in July, 1937.

Charles Dibdin

Charles Dibdin was a kind of nautical Irving Berlin whose songs are said to have boosted recruitment to the Royal Navy during the Napoleonic Wars and to have done much to improve sailors' morale. Dibdin, never one to hide his self-approval, put it like this: "My songs have been the solace of sailors in long voyages, in storms, in battle, and they have been quoted in mutinies to the restoration of order and discipline."

Yet the man who won fame in his lifetime and whose songs are still sung (though seldom by sailors) was strapped for cash most of his days. His complex and demanding love-life was part of the trouble; another was his propensity for quarrelling with his associates. The composer of *Tom Bowling* was forever in debt and finished up a bankrupt.

Charles Dibdin's life is a fascinating one. He was the son of Thomas Dibdin, parish clerk of Southampton's Holy Rood Church. In the shell of the blitzed building can still be seen a stone tablet recording the 1745 birth of his songwriting son. The setting is appropriate, for Dibdin wrote about sailors and the sea, and the ruined church is a memorial to the Merchant Navy.

Dibdin Senior was a High Street silversmith who sent his son to Winchester College in the hope that one day he would become a clergyman. But Winchester's choir developed his singing voice and when he left school Charles sang at soirees. His precosity and capacity for hard work saw him producing his own opera, *The Shepherd's Artifice,* at Covent Garden when he was a mere 17 years old.

Dibdin worked as an actor, composer and pro-

A commemorative plaque to Dibdin in the ruins of Holy Rood Church, now a Merchant Navy memorial.

ducer at Drury Lane for 12 years or more before he had one of his more important quarrels — with the famous actor-manager David Garrick. Another big name with which Dibdin was associated was the clown Grimaldi — their "harlequinades" led to the pantos of the present day.

Behind the writing of *Tom Bowling,* greatest and most enduring of his many hits, is a poignant story.

Dibdin had always loved the sea and his beloved elder brother Tom was a sailor. It was Captain Tom who persuaded Charles that wealth lay in India. So, believing that a stay there might relieve his frequent money problems, Charles set sail in 1788; but when a storm forced the ship to put in at Torquay he changed his mind and returned to London. Then came the sad news that Tom had died after being struck by lightning while crossing the Indian Ocean. The tragedy inspired *Tom Bowling.*

The song that became famous was featured at the Lyceum in the first of a series of one-man

His songs helped victories at sea

This statuette of Dibdin can also be seen at Tudor House — Echo photos.

or (from *Jack in his Element*) "In every mess I find a friend; In every port a wife."

Maybe Dibdin saw in a sailor's life that devotion to duty, that heroism, which was so lacking in his own improvident career, and envied those qualities. Whatever the merits of songs like *Tom Bowling* the sentiments were genuine enough to strike a chord not only with the generation for which it was written: "Faithful, below, he did his duty; but now he's gone aloft".

Charles Dibdin's spinet — presented by his descendants — in Tudon House Museum. His portrait (right) hangs above it.

shows. Dibdin recited, he acted, and he sang this and his other successes — songs like *Poor Jack* and *The Bells of Aberdovey*. But although the shows ran for 200 nights, the performer-composer remained short of money.

He thought his luck had changed when the Government granted him a £200 pension. But a new Prime Minister, Lord Greville, took it away in 1806—ironically, in view of Dibdin's contribution to the Navy, the year after the Battle of Trafalgar!

Next he went in for a music shop enterprise. This, too, proved a failure, but he was saved from destitution by a public subscription. In 1813 came illness and in July of the following year he died.

Descendants presented his spinet to Tudor House Museum close to his birthplace. Also there are a portrait and a statuette of the composer whose productivity was staggering: 900 songs, most of them nautical, and a hundred dramatic pieces with titles like *The Milkmaid*, *Tom Thumb* and *The Trip to Portsmouth*.

Dibdin's work, so popular in its day, strikes us now as too sentimental and patriotic to merit much of a revival in interest. Yet many of his lines live on. "The lass that loves a sailor," for example,

Lucia Foster Welch

"She has blazed a trail not only for the women of Southampton but for the women of the country, a trail it will be hard for those who come after to follow."

These were the words of the Rector of All Saints, Southampton, the Rev. J. R. Blennerhassett-West, at the funeral of Mrs. Lucia Marion Foster Welch, the suffragette who became the city's first woman mayor.

Lucia, who died in March, 1940, could boast, with pride, of a clutch of other local "firsts": first woman councillor, first woman alderman, first woman sheriff. She could also claim to have been Britain's first woman admiral — because the Mayor of Southampton also has the title Admiral of the Port — and at the time (1926) was believed to be the only woman in the United Kingdom to hold the office of sheriff.

It was appropriate that such a pioneer should also have been a supporter of women's suffrage. Mrs Foster Welch, a prominent Conservative, belonged both to the Women's Social and Political Union — the Suffragettes — and the National Union of Women's Suffrage Societies — the Suffragists.

What's more, she was an active supporter. When Mrs. Pankhurst came to speak at the Palace Theatre in Above Bar on February 4, 1911, Lucia invited friends and supporters of the WSPU to tea at her house, 61 Oxford Street (now a Cheshire Home), to meet the leader. She also offered hospitality for meetings to the NUWSS and when they learned, in September, 1912, that the Anti-Suffrage League were planning to concentrate that winter on Southampton she headed a campaign to counteract them.

Lucia Foster Welch, as befitted a doctor's wife and one whose mother had been a close friend of prison reformer Elizabeth Fry, had a lifelong interest in health and social welfare. During the Great War, operating from a Back-of-the-Walls school, she took charge of a scheme for feeding needy children — she had done similar work in Liverpool before she came to Southampton in 1903.

Frank Brook's Southampton Art Gallery portrait of Lucia Foster Welch.

Southampton's original "First Lady"

She was unflinching in her concern, too. When she became chairman of the civic health committee she sought out lecturers and helpers for educational propaganda on the dangers of venereal disease — and undertook much of the lecturing to women audiences herself.

On her death, early in the Second World War, the Daily Echo referred to two enduring memorials to her public work: the maternity ward at the Borough (now the General) Hospital and "the town's fine system of school clinics." But her interest in health was nation-wide — she was the first woman to serve on the Port Sanitary Association of the British Isles and was its president for two years. In the tradition of Elizabeth Fry, her mother's friend, Lucia Foster Welch was also a prison visitor. A JP from 1920, she was one of the first women magistrates to visit Winchester Prison.

She first became a councillor, as a representative for Newtown Ward, in 1918 and held the seat until she joined the aldermanic bench in 1928. In 1926, playing the town's customary pre-mayoral role, she became the only woman sheriff to be appointed in Southampton since the granting of the Charter by Henry VI in 1447. Her mayoral year, 1927, was an eventful and enjoyable one and she paid an official visit to the United States.

When this remarkable woman died on March 10, 1940, she left behind a poem she had written, to be read after her death. It went:

"No funeral gloom, my dears, when I am gone.
No tears, black raiment or graveyard grimness.
Think of me as withdrawn into the dimness.
　Yours still, you mine.

61 Oxford Street, once the home of the city's first woman mayor.

Remember all the best of our past moments and forget the rest.
And so, to where I wait, come gently on."

Though it was, traditionally a "black raiment" affair, one aspect of the civic funeral would have particularly pleased the lady for whom health work had been all-important — uniformed nurses walked in procession to All Saints Church behind the Mayor and Corporation.

Her daughter, the late Mrs Marion McHaffie, who had served as her mayoress, later described her mother as "a very determined lady" who had struggled against all the odds. She had believed that women would get the franchise through their own abilities — which is just what happened during the First World War when women took the place of men on the home front and proved their worth.

As her daughter always liked to point out, Mrs Foster Welch had never been the sort of suffrage campaigner to advocate breaking the law in the cause. But she was just as ardent in her way as the extremists. It's gratifying that she lived not only to see women get the vote but to see more and more of them play a wider rôle in public affairs.

Patrick Garland

There was something both precocious and immensely likeable about the teenage Patrick Garland. He got off to an impressive start, winning an *Observer* poetry competition when he was 18 with a poem in celebration of Sir Winston Churchill's 79th birthday. The next year, while still at St. Mary's College, Southampton, he was top of the contents list on the August cover of the *London Magazine*, followed by Laurie Lee, C. Day Lewis and Graham Greene, in that order! His contribution: verses about the poet John Clare.

These early successes didn't turn his head, though. And when he would join his friends for lunch in the restaurant of Edwin Jones' store and, with a broad grin, say things like "I've got to get back to give the headmaster his English lesson", he somehow never sounded conceited. Oblivious of such quips, the college authorities invited their former head boy back in 1981 to present the prizes. By this time, the ever-genial Patrick—who was now accompanied by a glamorous actress wife, Alexandra Bastedo—had become artistic director of the Chichester Festival Theatre.

In between leaving St. Mary's and that Southampton Guildhall speech day a great deal happened to the young poet who soon abandoned his laurel wreath for the masks of comedy and tragedy. It wasn't so surprising that Patrick, having been a keen amateur actor with the Southampton Student Players, should go in for the theatre after university. But acting was soon given up in favour of direction and literary adaptations for the stage.

The credits from the late Sixties are certainly impressive. They include directing two Alan Bennett plays *40 Years On* with Sir John Gielgud

Patrick Garland in 1989.   *Photo: Hamish Hamilton.*

(1968) and *Getting On* with Kenneth More (1970); his own adaptation of diarist John Aubrey's *Brief Lives*, with Roy Dotrice (1968); two films, *The Snow Goose* (1974) with Richard Harris and *A Doll's House* with Claire Bloom (a 1976 screen version of his Ibsen stage production); and *Billy*, a long-running Drury Lane musical.

One musical production he definitely wasn't happy about was *Hair*, which he did in Israel. It was, he said, "a most vivid experience"—in 1972 Israel was on the brink of war and *Hair* is about peace! If at any time he's unhappy about something he's done (he told a reporter in 1976) he could always say it was better than *Hair* . . .

Most of the time reviews of his work are favourable and, on occasion, enthusiastic, but there are exceptions—one was *Signed and Sealed*, a Feydeau farce with Kenneth Williams. Modest as ever, Patrick went on record as saying that the bad reviews were "cataclysmically right." Another musical he did dealt with the defrocked Southampton-born Rector of Stiffkey who figures elsewhere in this volume.

From the Southampton Student Players to the world stage

1978 saw Patrick Garland almost on home territory when he presented his version of Thomas Hardy's *Under the Greenwood Tree* at Salisbury Playhouse. Two years before he'd been talking of his hopes to get staged his adaptation of the Dorset novelist's novel about a church band in the early decades of the 19th Century. No company, from the National downwards, seemed interested. Why? Because all of them felt that it would be impossible to find a cast who played musical instruments.

But when he approached Salisbury Playhouse the then director, Roger Clissold, showed nothing but enthusiasm—particularly gratifying, this, because the first professional theatre the

A teenage Patrick Garland at a Southampton Theatre Guild ball with another local amateur player, Helen Wilson.

schoolboy Garland ever saw was the Salisbury arts company when they regularly visited Southampton's Avenue Hall. "Let's not look at the difficulties," Roger assured Patrick. "We'll make it work." And they did.

Seven actors who could sing and play musical instruments were found and after a successful run the production transferred to the Vaudeville Theatre in London. But Patrick was back at Salisbury a couple of years later with a humorous Caryl Brahms-Ned Sherrin show about Sir Thomas Beecham (played by Timothy West). This, too, transferred.

After a production of the York Mystery Plays came a visit to America where he directed a revival of *My Fair Lady*. Then, from 1980 until 1984, he occupied the shoes of Lord Olivier and other distinguished successors as Chichester Festival Theatre boss—a time which saw *Underneath the Arches*, the Flanagan and Allen musical he co-authored, going on to the West End. Some enterprises later came a right royal honour when his gala *Fanfare for Elizabeth* was presented in celebration of the Queens's 60th birthday.

1989 was an important year for Patrick. It marked the appearance, to enthusiastic reviews, of his first novel, *The Wings of the Morning* (inspired by his father's diary as a First World War fighter pilot), and his return both to Chichester and Thomas Hardy, charged with the mammoth task of recreating the Napoleonic Wars in *Victory*! his adaptation of the three-part epic verse drama *The Dynasts*. At least no lengthy commuting was involved, for the Garlands live not far away at Selsey, surrounded by a large collection of animals.

Nat Gonella

The young Nat Gonella at the height of his Thirties fame.

Nat Gonella's years of fame were the Thirties, an era which his distinctive Cockney vocals and trumpet style evoke. He had a renaissance in the Sixties and now enjoys a happy retirement in Gosport as a respected elder statesman of British jazz. But there were 13 Southampton years in the doldrums.

Nevertheless the chirpy Londoner looks back on those immediate post-war days as happy ones. He made a lot of friends in Southampton and enjoyed playing gigs with the local musicians. And, of course, at the Court Royal Hotel in Northlands Road, where he was playing in May, 1946, he met his wife Dorothy.

Cabby's son Nathaniel Charles Gonella, born on March 7, 1908, was brought up at Kings Cross. The family fell on hard times when the father died in 1915, at 44, and heartbroken Elizabeth Gonella was forced to send her three youngest children, including the seven-year-old Nat, into a home.

Like his hero and friend Louis Armstrong, Nat Gonella owes his career to learning an instrument in an institution, for it was while he was at St. Mary's Guardians School, Islington, that he took up the cornet under the tuition of a former regimental bandmaster, learning techniques he later passed on in his book *Modern Style Trumpet Playing*.

It was while working as a 15-year-old, 15-shillings-a-week errand boy that he bought his first cornet, priced £3.10s.—he put down five bob and paid the rest off at half-a-crown a week. Then one day in 1924 the new recruit to St. Pancras British Legion Brass Band answered an advert in *The Stage* for "young boys aged 16-18 who play

brass instruments." Nat passed the audition and joined Archie Pitt's Busby Boys.

Archie Pitt, of course, was the impresario husband of the up-and-coming young star Gracie Fields, a kindly lass who helped the Busby Boys with their routines and who one day gave Nat an old gramophone she was replacing. She included some jazz records. Nat was hooked . . .

The remainder of the decade found the young Gonella in the dance band world. By 1930 he was a featured soloist with the Billy Cotton band and had made his first recordings, and in the following year, as a member of the Roy Fox band, played for royalty—the Prince of Wales and the Duke of Kent among them—at the prestigious Monseigneur Restaurant in Piccadilly . Broadcasts and further visits to the recording studios followed. Now Nat was making a feature of a song the future Edward VIII regularly requested—Hoagy Carmichael's *Georgia On My Mind*, which was to become the Gonella signature tune.

1932 was a significant year for Nat: he made his first record under his own name and he met his idol, Louis Armstrong, who came over to play a

The lean Southampton years of "Britain's Louis Armstrong"

two-week engagement at the London Palladium. They met when Nat offered to return an overhauled trumpet to "Satchmo". They became friends and whenever Louis visited Britain in subsequent years his first question was invariably "Where's Nat?".

After leaving the Lew Stone band Nat Gonella at last formed his own band, the Georgians. They soon became a top attraction and in 1935 cut as many as 48 titles for the Parlophone record label— the following year the figure was 57 and in 1937 it was 64! Nat was a star of Variety: the Georgians were packing theatres throughout the land and there were even a couple of movies.

At the end of this golden decade came a visit to America, where Nat renewed his friendship with Louis and made some recordings with a group of American musicians, including the great alto saxophonist Benny Carter. He was never to reach such heights again. Certainly the war must have been a sobering financial experience—as a Pioneer Corps private his pay of ten bob net contrasted sadly with his previous income of £150 a week. But after playing in the Tank Regiment band during the Italian campaign, he was invalided out because of a duodenal ulcer and soon returned to bandleading and recording.

After the war Nat found himself in the town that was to be his home until the end of the Fifties. He played for two periods at Southampton's old Court Royal Hotel, where he met his third wife Dorothy. They bought a house off Woodmill Lane—18 Norwich Road—and stayed in the town for 13 years. He gigged around the nation (as well as locally), flirted unhappily with modern jazz, played summer seasons and in the early Fif-

ties returned to the variety stage, touring with Max Miller. Back home in Norwich Road, Nat would occasionally give trumpet lessons to aspiring young jazzmen, among them Mick Erridge of the long established Solent City Jazzmen.

"Britain's Louis Armstrong" was eventually reduced to playing in crummy clubs and the back rooms of pubs for a few pounds. But by 1959, when he left Southampton to live briefly in London and then Blackpool, a comeback was just round the corner. Nat made a well-received LP, *Salute to Satchmo*, and formed his last "Georgians," the Georgia Jazz Band, at the height of the boom in "trad" jazz. In 1960 Eamonn Andrews surprised him with the big red book on *This Is Your Life*.

Nat and Dorothy have retired to a cottage by the sea at Gosport, but their quiet life has been punctuated by bouts of media attention. He has been crowned King of Jazz in Holland and seen his biography published and his old records reissued, and Gosport Jazz Club celebrated his 80th birthday in style. Though he no longer plays the trumpet, on his occasional visits to jazz clubs he can usually be persuaded to sing the odd request. Including *Georgia*, of course.

Nat Gonella (right) in 1989, paying a vocal visit to a Sunday lunchtime session at the Brewery Bar, Botley. With him are former jazz promoter Bob Champion (left) and the author.

45

General Gordon

General Charles "Chinese" Gordon (1833-1885), the eccentric, puritanical soldier who died at the hands of the Mahdi, wasn't a Sotonian, but during 20 or so years of his life he looked upon 5 Rockstone Place, now the history department of La Sainte Union of Higher Education, as his home. His parents moved there when his father, Lieut.-General Henry Gordon, retired around 1857.

The 1861 cencus records that General and Mrs Gordon lived at the elegant Regency-style terrace house with their eldest daughter Augusta, then 39, and three servants. Gordon Junior stayed briefly on leave from time to time and in 1865 was there for several months, in retreat from the publicity surrounding his putting down of the Taiping Rebellion in China — his exploits had earned him the nickname of "Chinese" Gordon.

The general was a complex character whose self-effacement was sometimes cancelled out by bursts of intolerance and temper. At Woolwich Arsenal his commission was held back after he struck a fellow cadet with a clothes brush. But not long afterwards the strong religious convictions which never left him began to take hold. Gordon said of himself: "I have a wonderful instinct but very bad judgment."

In the depths of Gordon's soul, wrote Lytton Strachey in Eminent Victorians, were "intertwining contradictions — intricate recesses where egoism and renunciation melted into one another, where the flesh lost itself in the spirit and the spirit in the flesh."

Full of nervous energy like many another heavy smoker, the wiry warrior who read his Bible as assiduously as the Mahdi read the Koran, spent

General Gordon.

much of his time putting his Christianity into practice by helping the poor, especially street urchins.

This interest was reflected in the Gordon Boys Brigade which was set up after the general's death as a memorial to him, providing a corps of uniformed messengers and helping deserving poor boys find new opportunities overseas. Sadly, the building in Southampton's Ogle Road which was its headquarters (it closed in 1937) no longer exists — it was demolished by bulldozers in October, 1987, to make way for the new Heron development. The foundation stone, laid by

Southampton was home to the hero of Khartoum

Queen Victoria's daughter Princess Beatrice on August 10, 1889, and which might well have been saved and placed in another appropriate place, was deplorably, allowed to vanish amid the rubble.

After Gordon died at Khartoum — and there is more than one account of the manner of his death: his body was never found — his sister Augusta turned 5 Rockstone Place into a virtual Gordon museum, with mementoes and souvenirs, and items of exotica like a Nile crocodile and the "Sudan throne" (a simple, folding camp chair!).

There, too, was a teapot from which he poured cuppas for the under-privileged boys of Gravesend, where he spent six years superintending Thames defence works from 1865 until 1871. The house, which had been leased to the Gordons, was bought by the general for £900 in 1874 following the death of his mother (his father died in 1865) and remained in the ownership of the family until 1919.

Augusta lived there until her own death in 1893, when it passed to their younger sister Helen, widow of Gordon's surgeon in China, Dr Moffitt. Helen was still there at the time of her death 26 years later.

As a result of an article on Gordon's local connections by A. G. K. Leonard (Hampshire County Magazine, 1981) the general was to be seen again at No. 5 — in the person of actor Robert Hardy, playing him on location for a BBC television documentary.

Other associations with the hero of Khartoum can be found in dockland's Queens Park, where there's a memorial to him — four marble columns on a granite block, surmounted by a cross — and at the Old Cemetery on the Common. Here, one

Gordon's Southampton home, 5 Rockstone Place.

of the panels on the tomb of General Henry Gordon, his wife Elizabeth and their children refers to "Charles George, born at Woolwich, January 28, 1833, slain at Khartoum January 26, 1885". But one other local memorial didn't meet with the approval of sister Helen.

Twenty-five years after her brother's death, Alderman Edward Wise, a former Mayor of Southampton, gave a window at St Luke's Church where Gordon had his last Communion in England before leaving for his final mission in the Sudan. Mrs Moffitt objected to the inclusion in the design of another figure apart from her brother — that of the donor, standing in mayoral garb beneath the general! A bishop duly replaced the figure of Wise. The window is now at the Gordon Boys School near Woking.

Maundy Gregory

When Maundy Gregory put on his new (and only) play, *Self-Condemned*, at Southampton's Philharmonic Hall on August 1, 1898, the religious drama was excellently costumed — the vestments and church ornaments, including a medieval brass lectern, had been borrowed from St Michael's Church without the permission of the Vicar, his father. It was an early indication of his enterprising son's eye to the main chance.

The man who would later be jailed for dealing in honours had an early brush with the law in 1909 during his career as a theatrical impresario. His panto *Little Red Riding Hood* at the Lyceum, Ipswich, was built around a seven-year-old girl and Maundy was fined a fiver for allowing her to appear in contravention of the Prevention of Cruelty to Children Act.

Then there was the occasion when the unpaid musicians taking part in a comic opera called *Dorothy*, presented by "Messrs. Maundy-Gergory", went on strike at a theatre in the Strand. Maundy rushed to the basement, pulled the mains switch, plunged the audience into darkness and explained that there had been an electricity failure, something indignantly denied by the Charing Cross Electricity Supply Company! This marked the end of a theatrical career which had begun in Maundy's native town at the turn of the century, but there was drama to come on a much more extravagant scale than anything depicted in Gregory's own productions.

He was born in Portland Terrace in July, 1877, to the Rev. Francis Gregory and his wife Ursula. Father Gregory was the man whose introduction of High Church ideas into this working class parish didn't initially go down all that well.

Like his son he was a controversial figure. Religion played a large part in Maundy's own career, something which would have deeply shocked his father had he lived to see it. After his dealing in political honours had begun to decline, Maundy, who had converted to Roman Catholicism, concentrated on the obtaining of papal privileges.

But long before all that Maundy had moved on from the theatre to try his hand at publishing. His magazine Mayfair, unlike its present-day namesake, offered society news. There was also a feature called Man of the Day (later Men of the Twentieth Century). According to Tom Cullen in his delightful biography *Maundy Gregory: Purveyor of Honours* (the Bodley Head, 1974), such Men contributed anything from 50 to 500 guineas

His father's church, St. Michael's.

48

Prince of Con Men

Maundy Gregory: honours and dishonour.

for the privilege of inclusion. The prince of con men was on his way.

The song parody *Lloyd George Knew My Father* refers to the "jobs for the boys" corruption rife at the time of the Welsh Wizard's post-war Government. Lloyd George needed large sums of money to fight the 1918 election and one sure way of raising fortunes was through bartering honours for contributions. An honours broker was needed, and Maundy Gregory fitted the bill. The shrewd Sotonian's cover was the Whitehall Gazette which looked more like an official Government publication than a magazine. And, as with Mayfair, those profiled therein forked out for the privilege.

From the late Twenties Gregory owned the Ambassador Club, which became a well-known rendezvous for parliamentarians at lunch-times. By night it turned into a haunt of royalty, society figures and artists. Gregory's connections remained useful even though the honours business had largely come to an end with the fall of

Lloyd George and the sale of honours had, through the passing of the Honours (Prevention of Abuses) Act, become a criminal offence.

Maundy made other purchases: a luxurious hotel in Dorking and *Burke's Landed Gentry*. He also became a professional fund-raiser and found, too, that business in papal honours was a profitable sideline. Gregory put it about that he could fix things with the Vatican. In 1932 John Farrow, later a top Hollywood director, husband of Maureen O'Sullivan and father of Mia Farrow, was anxious to get a marriage annulment and narrowly avoided being conned out of £500 by Gregory who had offered to arrange it.

The Thirties saw a decline in Maundy's fortunes. After a disastrous settlement when the executors of an estate sued him to recover £30,000, "the cheerful giver" (as Lord Birkenhead had called him) found himself in financial difficulties. There were overheads at the Ambassador Club and trouble at the Dorking hotel.

In 1932 his friend Mrs Rosse — they were more like brother and sister than lovers, since Maundy was homosexual — died in mysterious circumstances, leaving him a covenient £18,000. Many considered it unlikely that Maundy had murdered her, though the investigating chief inspector had his doubts.

Maundy's own end was not all that far away. The following year he offered a knighthood for £10,000 to a man who didn't want it, a trial and a two-month prison term followed and Maundy went into exile in France. He left on April 12, 1933, and never returned, dying during the Occupation in 1941. Grandiloquent to the last, he had given himself a knighthood!

"Uncle George" (Michael Hannides)

The story of Michael George Hannides reads like a folk tale. America was built by men like him, hard-workers who would rise at dawn and still be toiling when others were slipping down beneath the covers. But, instead of going to America to fulfil his dream of making good, Michael left his native village to settle in Southampton where he was to become one of its most prominent and respected citizens and leader of the Cypriot community.

"I suppose I must be the Godfather," grins the semi-retired restaurateur, but no more respectable and cheerful a Godfather than this portly 75-year-old could be imagined. His life has turned out well, but the beginnings in his sunny island were inauspicious — hunger was seldom far away. So in 1936, just into his twenties, Michael sailed for Britain with his friend, the late Nick Lysandrides, to seek his fortune.

Michael and Nick, who had lived next door to each other and had even shared mother's milk, slept in the cool of the ship's deck while first class passengers perspired in their cabins. On their arrival Nick set out for Clacton, where he eventually opened a restaurant, and Michael, who at this time spoke hardly any English, plumped for Southampton where he was employed as a mobile ice cream man for the princely sum of sixpence a day.

He didn't stay long in the job. Off he went to London to work as a baker, though his ambition was to become a carpenter. He became one, too — in Wales, where he not only perfected his English, but learnt Welsh. The occasional Welsh-speaking visitors to George's Restaurant in downtown Southampton usually react with amazement when Michael joins in the conversation in their native tongue. . . .

By 1939 Michael had prospered enough to launch his restaurant in the shadow of Southampton's oldest building, St Michael's Church. Here he laboured hard, putting in all the hours God made for many years and providing dishes like his legendary Spaghetti with Meat Balls to a varied clientele which included solicitors like Coroner Harfield and merchant seamen like teenage star-to-be Tommy Steele.

Michael is full of stories about the customers of those early days, recounting how he staked some skint ones to a free meal and how they never

One day in 1936 the 21-year-old Michael Hannides was photographed selling ice cream in Chapel. Fifty-two years later the Southern Evening Echo published the picture, with the result that Michael had an ice-cream reunion with one of the young customers — Mrs Bella Holmes, here seen on Michael's left On the right is Mrs Louise Lodgwidge, widow of a lad in the 1936 photo. Behind them is Michael's son Chris. Photo: Southern Newspapers.

The poor Cypriot boy who made good in his adopted town

forgot. Then there was the chap who ran out without paying — he later became a millionaire!

Road developments meant that the old restaurant building would have to go. Michael then opened bigger and better premises in a similar position, putting his old trade as a "chippie" to good use by making tables for the new "George's."

By this time the city's Cypriot community had grown. Many of its members were Michael's relatives and friends and from his native Koma tou Yialou (it means "village by the sea") at the far eastern tip of Cyprus. Several of them set up in business as restaurateurs. And for years now, of course, the community has had its own Greek Orthodox Church of St Nicolas in Bernard Street (formerly the Anglican church of St James).

Michael married late — he had been so busy building up his business that he hadn't bothered about looking for a wife. When he wed Charalampia, though, he made up for lost time and rather rapidly began to establish his dynasty. This most Greek of philosophers then reached a momentous decision: he would retire to devote his time to his family.

They've turned out remarkably well. Eldest son George is an accountant, Nick is a solicitor, Peter and Chris have taken over the restaurant (though Michael is there most mornings), John is a businessman and only daughter Mareca has gone in for fashion design.

In 1986, when Michael was 72, he decided to celebrate his half a century in his adopted city with a slap-up do at the restaurant. Nick Lysandrides, his immigrant friend from Clacton, was there. So was Michael's closest pal Lord Maybray-King, whose best man he had been.

George's Restaurant.

The former Speaker of the House of Commons spoke of Michael's one-time plan to build a hotel in Koma tou Yialou — a dream which the Turkish invasion shattered. The village remains in Turkish hands — something that casts a shadow over the happiness of all its expatriate sons and daughters, several of whom had wanted to retire to that idyllic spot. None is sadder than Michael Hannides.

Michael, known to everyone as "Uncle George", is noted for his wisdom and his aphorisms. The man who made a success of his business by rarely leaving it declared: "You can't drive a car sitting in the back seat." Why did he retire early? Michael replies to this one with another question: "What is the point of being a rich man in a graveyard?" And, of course, there's no answer to that. . . .

Henry Robinson Hartley

Students of Southampton University might be amused to learn that their founder was in favour of having a harem to himself — "plurality of women," he called it — and suffered lifelong ill-health as a result of venereal disease. It's doubtful that the young men and women who study there today would be shocked that Henry Robinson Hartley was a sexual rebel . . . though of course the ideas he advocated were popular with some intellectuals even in his day.

But it's pretty certain that Hartley himself would be shocked at the way in which the wishes he expressed in his will haven't turned out the way he wanted, for this unhappy eccentric hadn't envisaged a university. The scholar and naturalist who had once expressed highly unorthodox views had in mind a library for the "select scientific public", together with a garden, observatory, and collections relating to specified sciences.

The city fathers looked on the bequest as representing an opportunity for the progress and betterment of mankind and of Southampton in particular. So they pulled down Hartley's houses, burned his manuscripts (which they considered "obscene and blasphemous") and put up a building in High Street to keep his books. Out of this came a college bearing his name — the Hartley Institution. The college became a university college and the university college a university proper.

The life of Henry Robinson Hartley (1777-1850) was one of frustration, disillusionment, pain and sadness. The son and heir of a wine merchant whose family fortunes were made in the latter stages of the Eighteenth Century (a time of the town's prosperity as a spa and of a revival in the

The only known portrait of Henry Robinson Hartley. The unidentified painter's subject was nine at the time.

wine trade), he developed revolutionary and atheistical ideas which were anathema to society and business circles.

It is said that Henry James Pye of Little Testwood House, a man who would become the most respectable and the dullest of Poet Laureates, was his godfather — Pye had become an honorary burgess in 1776 at the end of the second mayoral term of Henry's father.

Alexander Anderson, in his biographical study *Hartleyana* (Scottish Academic Press and Southampton University, 1987), suggests that Henry's

Unwitting founder of Southampton University

rejection of Christianity may have had its roots in strict religious teaching at home and school, though Anderson records that Hartley spoke glowingly in letters of the advantages his days at the Grammar School of Southampton in Bugle Street had given him.

Hartley was content to lead an adult life not so much of leisure as scholarship: his time was taken up principally with study and writing. But though fearful of journeys and generally shy and retiring, he was stricken with strong sexual desires. One woman was not enough, apparently: he wanted "many at once."

Marriage to a girl named Celia Crowcher was solemnised at Portsea in 1798, but it was not a success and led to an annulment in 1802. From 1805 until 1809 the embittered young man's aim was "a short course of violent ecstatic pleasure", an interlude which probably unfolded in London rather than his birthplace and which saw a deterioration in his health, probably due to untreated gonorrhoea.

During this time Hartley wrote a lengthy document on lost opportunities which began with the words *"On such Picturesque as might possibly have been realised."* Hartley, who had been disinherited, looked at the life he might have led had his father died earlier than 1800. He muses on the sensual opportunities offered by travel to the Orient — "the unavoidable difficulties of having plurality of females here in Gothic Society, and the ease with which it may be obtained in Turkey, Persia, etc., etc., would have been an irresistible and most natural inducement."

His pipe-dream of setting up, in Turkey or America, a seraglio of women from all over the world, "always ready, and as companions and playfellows in Gardens & Houses", wouldn't have appealed to the feminists of "his" university, but such plans were very much in accord with the cries for a life of liberty which were being heard in those days of revolutionary ideas.

Hartley's desires were not to see fruition and he settled down to a life of reflection, the study of natural history, book collecting and the keeping of a journal. With his mother's death in 1821 his financial constraints came to an end, but the loss of a legal case over a dispute with a neighbour prompted his departure from High Street in 1824 to settle in Calais. There he died, as unhappy and as embittered as ever. But Henry Robinson Hartley isn't forgotten, for the University is his unexpected memorial.

The Robinson Hartley houses, 65-67 High Street, circa 1858.
Photos: Southampton University.

53

Sir Hubert Herkomer

"Sir Hubert who?," I hear you cry. The Bavarian-born painter who was brought up in Southampton has undergone a decline in reputation mainly due to his being in step with his own time but out of step with ours. As art critic William Gaunt wrote in *Victorian Olympus* (Jonathan Cape, 1952), Herkomer's success was won by piety and sentiment, qualities appreciated in Victorian and, to a lesser extent, Edwardian times but often sources of aesthetic embarrassment today.

The pathos conspicuous in his "greatest hit", *The Last Muster* (1874), a study of Chelsea Pensioners, was so successful that every member of the Royal Academy Selection Committee burst into spontaneous applause when it was shown to them! Viewed today, it looks presciently cinematic — like a scene from D. W. Griffith.

One is reminded that Herkomer, as well as being painter, architect, etcher and engraver, playwright, actor and dancer, composer, lecturer and teacher, was a pioneer of cinema. He built his own film studios at Bushey, where he ran a school of art during his years of fame, and before his death in 1914 produced a number of forgotten films (the film studios at Bushey are said to be the oldest still operating in Europe).

Herkomer was in fact more innovative than his conventional paintings might suggest. Little has been written about Herkomer's theatrical design experiments, but they were certainly a great influence on the young Gordon Craig whose own scenic ideas were, in turn, to influence generations of designers who followed him. When he was 20, in 1892, Craig heard Herkomer attack such conventions as footlights — for casting shadows on

Sir Hubert Herkomer: a self-portrait.

actors' faces — and curtain raising — for revealing their feet first. . . .

At his little theatre in Bushey, where he presented his own plays accompanied by his own music, Herkomer suggested moving mists and clouds, at dawn or by moonlight, through the use of electric lights and painted gauzes. There were no footlights, only sidelights at a distance; much of the scenery was in relief; and the curtains parted slowly from the centre outwards. Craig, who had been to Herkomer's theatre with his mother, Ellen Terry, determined that if ever he became an actor-manager he would follow Herkomer's example and do away with footlights, open his curtains sideways and use electric light. (I am indebted to Edward Craig's 1968 Gollancz biography of his father for his comments on a none too well-known

"Truth in art should be enhanced by sentiment" —Herkomer

aspect of Herkomer's multi-faceted career).

The artist's parents brought their small son to Southampton, after a brief spell in America, in 1857. His woodcarver father Lorenz, whose portrait by his son is one of eight Herkomer paintings in the Southampton Art Gallery collection, had noted that the citizens looked well-dressed and thus likely to be good patrons of art. The experience proved to the contrary and for some time the family had to depend on the music lessons given by "Madame Herkomer" at their first home, 10 Windsor Terrace (demolished in 1936 to make way for the bus station which has been demolished in its turn). Later they moved to 1 Beckford Terrace, Manchester Street.

The young Hubert, like his Portland Street cousins the Verne sisters (who also appear in this book), showed musical ability but he decided on a career in art, initially attending the Southampton school before completing his studies in London. By 1873, the year one of his paintings was accepted by the Royal Academy, he was doing well enough to be able to settle his parents in a small cottage at Bushey.

Two years later *The Last Muster* was sold for £1,200 and made him famous. It later won him a gold medal at an international exhibition in Paris . . . where, it's interesting to record, Herkomer and Southampton-born painter Millais were the only two Englishmen to win distinction.

The painter's later years brought him substantial fees for portraits of the famous, among them Wagner and Tennyson. He became an ARA, an RA, opened his art school in Bushey and in 1885 succeeded Ruskin, no less, as Slade Professor of Fine Art at Oxford.

Herkomer, who gave up the Slade professorship in 1894, was in 1899 recognised by the land of his birth. The now internationally famous painter, born in Germany in 1849 but a naturalised Briton since he was 22, was made a member of a noble German order which allowed him to add "von" to his surname. But his greatest honour came in 1907 when he was knighted.

Three years later he called at his old home in Windsor Terrace to present the occupiers with an autographed copy of his new book, *The Herkomers*. But his last visit to the town of his childhood was in October, 1913, six months before his death, when he gave a talk at his alma mater, Southampton School of Art (then at the West Marlands), on his "latest love" — cinematography.

Sir Hubert left behind a widow — both his first two wives died — and a remarkable legacy at Bushey: a magnificent "castle" in the Bavarian baronial style which, sadly, was demolished early in the Second World War, not long after the Herkomer estate had to be wound up.

Long gone Herkomer House in Windsor Terrace, where Sir Hubert lived as a boy. Photo: Southampton Museums.

55

Benny Hill

His Westrow Gardens home.

It was as cold and cheerless a Christmas Day as the one in the workhouse poem. On the icy kitchen table lay the remains of the festive feast — bangers and mash. Buckets and bowls of water covered the floor. For this was the winter of 1986, the pipes had frozen and the householder had been forced to shave in the same water in which he had boiled his breakfast egg.

But as his neighbours pulled crackers behind windows twinkling with fairy lights, the lone occupant of the modest Southampton semi settled down in front of the telly to sip his sole concession to seasonal cheer, a chartreuse liqueur. Alfred Hawthorn Hill — as Mrs. Alice Moore, his Westrow Gardens neighbour, has pointed out — could have spent Christmas in luxury beneath the sun anywhere he chose.

The man the world knows as Benny Hill may well be less complex than he seems to his fans, most of whom are puzzled by his simple life style. But to someone who knows him better than most, his producer Dennis Kirkland, Benny is just "a very ordinary bloke with very ordinary tastes." Nevertheless, it seems strange to glimpse a multi-millionaire shopping with a plastic bag in Bedford Place, queueing up in a local takeaway or hopping on to a bus.

Sometimes the apparent asceticism seems to tremble on the edge of parody. When his biographer John Smith first wrote to him about his proposed book, Benny replied on a piece of exercise book paper. Unsurprisingly, the self-effacing comic wasn't too pleased about the prospect, his excuse being that one day he intended to write his autobiography.

Attempts by the tabliod press to dig up some dirt on this particular celebrity seemed doomed. The lifelong bachelor remains a scandal-free, private, solitary man who never appears on chat shows and never as a guest on the programmes of his fellow stars.

Not that Benny Hill has any need to do anything more than his three shows a year. Though his is a talent that some find too predictably leering and corny, it appears to have an enviable international appeal. From Connecticut to Cannes, Hill's popularity has shown little signs of abating: but if his fame died tomorrow, Benny Hill, the former milkman, could live for the rest of his life in the plush comfort he doesn't seem to need.

Certainly the beginnings had been modest. Benny's father, Alfred Senior, a one-time part-time clown in Bertram Mills' Circus, was manager of a surgical goods store in Canal Walk in downtown Southampton. It was a steady job to have in the (for some) hungry Thirties, but Dad was careful with the cash. Later his son (born in 1924) was to admit, illuminatingly: "The fact that I've never really enjoyed spending money has something to do with my upbringing. We were a very frugal family who, without being mean, always counted the pennies."

The lad from Westrow Gardens so loved the family outings to see the music hall stars at the Place in Above Bar or the Hippodrome in Ogle Road that the seed planted on Wednesday nights

The wag from Westrow Gardens

soon flowered. While still a scholarship boy at Taunton's he joined a concert party, then another at Eastleigh where he had become a horse-driving milkman for Hann and Son's dairy (a time which was to inspire Benny's greatest hit, *Ernie the Fastest Milkman in the West*).

After *Stars in Battledress* at the end of the war, Benny did the working men's club circuits, cabarets and touring shows, but it was burgeoning television which made his name. The first *Benny Hill Show* went out in January, 1955, though admittedly to unenthusiastic reviews. By 1970 it was watched in 9.25 million homes.

The world was soon tuning into Chow Mein the Chinaman, the Bavarian Professor Otto Stumpf, avant-garde film director Pierre de Terre and, of course, Fred Scuttle, his peak cap askew on his jolly moon face, blinking through wire-rimmed glasses and saluting in that endearingly servile way.

Americans in particular took to the cast of madcap characters and many nations world-wide responded to the silent comedy routines. I remember having to wait a long time for a drink in a Dieppe hotel because the patron and his family were gathered round the TV set chortling at Benny Hill.

"King Leer" strikes many as a mysteriously revered, repetitive and old-fashioned comic. But obviously the spirit of red-nosed music hall is not yet dead. Prisoners at a Californian "pen" threatened a riot in 1982 unless they could watch the Benny Hill Show . . . amazing, until you read that after ten years it still holds huge audiences coast to coast. British critic Michael Billington summed it up: "His popularity on American television is probably the most unexpected conquest of the continent since the Pilgrims landed at Plymouth Rock."

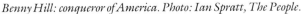

Benny Hill: conqueror of America. Photo: Ian Spratt, The People.

Baroness Hooper

When Gloria Dorothy Hooper was ten years old she won a scholarship audition to the Sadler's Wells ballet school. But the prospect of Gloria Hooperova starring in Swan Lake never got beyond the dream stage. She decided against a dancing career and thus Energy Minister Cecil Parkinson wasn't denied his unusually gifted Parliamentary under Secretary of State.

The multi-lingual lawyer, who at 45 became the youngest-ever life peer to take a seat in the House of Lords, is the perfect example of the local girl who made good. She was born in Hill Lane, Southampton, in 1939, went to the old Convent High School and took her degree at the university. But she is not, regrettably, Baroness Hooper of Southampton but of Liverpool — she represented that city in the European Parliament from 1978 until 1984.

After graduating in law, Gloria became tourist and information officer for Winchester, a job in which her ability in languages — French and Spanish, plus some Italian and German — proved an asset. That was in 1963. Two years later a great opportunity came her way.

Gloria, a member of Middle Temple hoping to be called to the Bar, had not long previously obtained a certificate in international law at Madrid University. There she had followed a course on Latin American political and economic organisations, so it was apt that when she won a Rotary Foundation Fellowship for International Understanding she should have chosen to spend an academic year in either Venezuela or Ecuador. As it happened, she found herself studying her pet subject — public international law — at the Central University in Quito, Ecuador.

Lady Hooper.

It was a memorable year: she spoke — in Spanish, of course — at Rotary clubs and gave talks to schools, was hospitalised with hepatitis, and witnessed a revolution! She also travelled on the highest motorway in Peru, crossed the country's highest lake in a British steamer and visited every country in South America by car, boat and aeroplane.

When she returned to her job in Winchester she gave no less than 60 talks — not only on her year's study but on the city she was employed to promote. In due course, having been admitted to the Law Society as a solicitor, she moved into the world of law and international commerce.

The local girl who became the youngest life peer

But politics had always played an important part in the lives of both Gloria and her elder sister Angela. Gloria had been president of Southampton University Conservative Association and secretary of Eastleigh Young Conservative Association. Angela was to become that division's Tory agent.

In 1978 Gloria stood as MEP for Liverpool and held the seat until 1984, becoming vice-chairman of the Committee on Environment, Public Health and Consumer Protection and, in 1983, deputy chief whip of the European Democratic Group. She also served on the ad hoc committee inquiring into "the situation of women" and was involved in various initiatives concerning inner cities as well as retailing.

In 1985, adopting the rather grandiose title of the Baroness Hooper, of Liverpool, and of St James's in the City of Westminster, she became one of 12 new peers announced by Mrs Thatcher. She took her seat in the Lords in June and by September of that year had become a Government Whip — as well as a baroness-in-waiting to the Queen.

While a Whip she was spokesman for education and science, the Foreign and Commonwealth Office and environment. There was further promotion for Lady Hooper in June, 1987, when she was appointed Parliamentary Under Secretary of State at the Department of Education and Science, with ministerial responsibility for non-advanced further education, inner cities, "education for a multi-cultural society", youth service, and internationl work.

In July, 1988, the Baroness was switched to another under secretaryship, this time at the Department of Energy, with special responsibility for energy efficiency and renewable sources of energy and for the handling of all departmental business in the House of Lords.

March 6, 1989, must have been a proud day for this talented daughter of a former Canadian Pacific Line commodore chief engineer. She was invited back to her home town university to give the 25th Hartley Memorial lecture — The Role of Government Today.

Lady Hooper, whose three years at the university had been, she readily admitted, all-important, told her audience that, in view of the longevity of members of the House of Lords, she hoped to be around to attend the 50th Hartley Lecture. Quipped the Vice-Chancellor (Dr Gordon Higginson): "We'll probably invite you to deliver it!"

Baroness Hooper's old school, the Convent High, in 1905.

59

Admiral "Jack" Jellicoe

Churchill, never a man to mince matters, said that Admiral Sir John Jellicoe was "the only man who could have lost the war in an afternoon." Earl Jellicoe, as the Southampton-born sailor became, spent his remaining years in the shadow of the Battle of Jutland — on May 31, 1916, three British battle cruisers, three cruisers and eight other ships went to the bottom of the North Sea and over 6,000 British tars perished. The Germans lost only 2,000.

Yet some naval historians have since contended that criticisms of Jellicoe were unfair. There had been no precedent for such a large-scale engagement, for one thing, and the Germans held the initiative from the start. Jellicoe, blamed for caution, said his objective was to discourage the German Navy from going out in strength again . . . and it certainly worked. The question remains: could any other commander have done better?

By the end of the year Admiral Beatty had taken over the command of the Fleet. Jellicoe was briefly First Sea Lord. Then, from 1920 until 1924, he was Governor-General of New Zealand and five years later became an earl.

On March 27, 1929, his native town gave him the Freedom of the Borough at the new Empire Theatre (now the Mayflower). No resentment over Jutland seems to have been felt by his fellow townsfolk — they cheered him along the route of his ceremonial carriage drive from the Docks, where he had been honoured with a special lunch aboard the liner Olympic.

Despite the controversy and the unwanted publicity that had followed the battle, Jellicoe was treated as the hero he undoubtedly was — he had seen action at the bombardment of Alexandria in

Earl Jellicoe (centre) with the Mayor of Southampton aboard the Olympic on March 29, 1929 — the day the old seadog was given the Freedom of his native Borough.

The spectre of Jutland haunts his name still

1882, was aboard HMS Victoria when she sank in the Med., and during the Boxer Rebellion, when he was sent to relieve besieged legations at Peking, was severely wounded. As far back as the Eighties, while gunnery lieutenant on HMS Monarch, he rescued a bluejacket who had fallen overboard in a gale.

Like Nelson, "Jack" Jellicoe was short of stature. And like the hero of Trafalgar, he wasn't unduly modest. When he gained a place in the training ship Britannia in 1872 he inscribed one of his books as "the property of Admiral Sir John Jellicoe". A lad determined to get on. . . .

The sea was in his blood. His father was a skipper and later a commander of the Royal Mail Steam Packet Company, and a grandfather of his mother had been Second Sea Lord at the time of Trafalgar.

At the time of his birth the Jellicoes were living in High Street, though they later moved to Anglesea Place, off Above Bar, and then to East Park Terrace. After schooling at Southampton's Banister Court and in Brighton, he took to the Navy like a duck to water and at 18 had sailed the world. He'd always loved the sea, of course. He and his brothers Herbert and Edward (later Rector of Freemantle) were keen on sailing and spent much of their spare time on or near the water.

Gunnery was his speciality. In 1883 he won an £80 prize for it and by 1907, when he had completed a two-year term as Director of Naval Ordnance, was credited with improving the navy's firing abilities. Between 1907 and 1911 he had risen successively to Rear Admiral, Lord Commander and Controller of the Navy, Vice Admiral

The Mayflower, once the new Empire Theatre where Jellicoe was given his Freedom.

and Commander of the Atlantic Fleet. And in 1912 he followed in the rolling gait of his maternal great-grandfather by becoming Second Sea Lord.

When the Great War broke out Jellicoe found himself in command of the Grand Fleet and was promoted Admiral in 1915. Then came Jutland.

Learning through an intercepted message that the German navy had decided to strike, Jellicoe put into action a plan involving his battleships and Admiral Beatty's battle cruisers. Certainly the battle, which involved such tragic losses on the British side, was no victory. It was not a decisive affair, but it did discourage the enemy from similar ventures — Jellicoe's idea all along.

In 1935 — ironically on Armistice Day — Southampton's most famous sailor caught a chill while paying tribute to the dead of the Great War at London's Cenotaph. Nine days later he died of pneumonia and was laid to rest in St. Paul's . . . close to Nelson.

Sir Sidney Kimber

Sidney Kimber may have been stocky in stature but in other ways he was a giant. Between the wars he strode Southampton like a Colossus: a ruthless man of vision whose memorials are the Civic Centre and the Sports Centre, both of which were vigorously opposed when plans were first put forward.

Kimber was not a man to trifle with and expected to have things done his way. His motto: If you want something done, do it yourself. He despised academics, particularly Arts men, reserving his approval for technical people who could put their talents to practical use. Scorn he regarded as a useful weapon; and when, during the heat of Council debates, he was on the receiving end of Labour attacks, he just roared with laughter.

Southampton's most memorable politician this century was born in 1873 and from 1884 to 1889 was at King Edward V. School, leaving at 14 to go into his father's business—Kimber Senior was a schoolteacher turned brickmaker whose business operated in Highfield on the site of present-day University buildings. In 1900, when he was 27, Sidney inherited the business (which later became a building firm).

In the Nineties he had joined Portswood Conservative Association and was elected to the Borough Council in 1910, becoming an alderman in 1916. The following year he became Sheriff—the usual prelude to the mayoralty. In November, 1918, as mayor for the first of two terms, he announced the end of the war to the citizens from the balcony of the High Street Audit House where the Council met (it was blitzed in 1940).

"The effect was instantaneous," Kimber wrote in his autobiography, *Thirty Eight Years of Public*

Life in Southampton. "The crowd went stark, staring mad with emotion and delirium. Hats, gloves, newspapers, matchboxes were thrown in the air, cheering was spontaneous and men and women's eyes were moist and wet with streaming happy tears."

Kimber was particularly delighted that he could now get on with plans to build a town hall and municipal offices on the West Marlands, plans that the war had interrupted. There were some dissentient voices in his own party opposed to anything of a grandiose nature which might lead to a rates increase, and of course his arch enemies in the Labour group, notably its leader "Tommy" Lewis, felt that if money was to be spent in such a lavish way it should be on the people rather than on ostentatious civic buildings. But in 1928 he made a pact with "Tommy"—Labour undertook

The Civic Centre viewed from Sir Sidney's beloved Rose Garden. What would the old boy think of its disappearance?
Photo: Southern Newspapers.

A portrait of Sir Sidney presented anonymously in 1939, the work of T. C. Dugdale, RA (1880-1952).

Photo: Southampton Art Gallery.

to drop their opposition in return for the Corporation building 2,000 houses.

There were other concessions. Under the Civic Centre Bill the Corporation agreed to provide elsewhere an amount of recreational space equivalent to that of the lost playground of the Marlands. But Kimber's lengthy battle was won and the old warrior must have been a proud man when the future George VI laid the foundation stone in 1930. The municipal offices came first in 1932, then the Law Courts in 1933, the Guildhall in 1937 and the Central Library and the School of Art, blitzed two years later, in 1939.

· The critics still droned on. The Civic Centre was too big, too expensive. They continued to complain with Kimber's next brainchild, the Sports Centre. The pugnacious alderman had fought for years to get better sports facilities for the town, and after ten years of battle, doubtless relished by him, Lordswood farmland was bought and turned into the fulfilment of another Kimber dream. "A white elephant," snapped "Tommy" Lewis when it was opened in 1938 . . .

"Vote for Kimber—who says what he thinks and means what he says". That was one of his election slogans, and undoubtedly there was truth in it. Professor A. Temple Patterson, in his book *Southampton: A Biography,* tells us that Kimber, "originally an unprogressive Conservative opposed to municipal enterprise because he believed that, in his own words, 'most of the undertakings would be better in the hands of private people,' became a convert to municipalisation." One wonders how he would have got on with Margaret Thatcher.

His record as a servant of the people was recognised by a knighthood in 1935. But he didn't resign from the Council until 1948, the year before his death, after 38 years of continuous service to the borough—he was Mayor twice, in 1918 and 1919.

Kimber was a man much admired and much disliked. But you felt that even some opponents had a grudging liking for what one ex-councillor called "an old so-and-so." He had a loud voice and a personality to match. But he saw the future and was determined to make it work.

Richard Cockle Lucas

Had the sculptor Richard Cockle Lucas lived to see *Peter Pan,* he would have shouted a hearty "Yes!" to the question "Do you believe in fairies?" For not only did he commune with the little people—he even "married" one, and wrote about it in his old age.

Mind you, R. C. L. wasn't like normal men. Even in Victorian times when, it seems, eccentrics were thicker on the ground than they are today, he stood out. Few people before or since have driven through the streets of Southampton in a Roman-style chariot, standing erect with a long toga flapping behind them. For Richard Cockle Lucas every day was Carnival Day.

Lucas, best known for that statue of hymn-writer Isaac Watts so much admired by pigeons and public in Southampton's West Park, was born in Salisbury in 1800, the son of a cloth manufacturer, and first encountered the fairy world when his wicked stepmother locked him in the cider cellar.

But, stay, who is that little fellow in the knee breeches and the tailcoat? Step forward, Roger Diddums, an emissary from the fairy king himself. Through this amiable gnome, Little Dick (as the elderly sculptor called his youthful self) soon comes to know the members of the fairy court. He also learns, from the lips of the maiden herself, that his girl friend Hetty Lottie, with whom he had gone through a make-believe marriage ceremony conducted by a playful mill worker, is really a fairy.

Years pass, Hetty sadly dies, Little Dick becomes a well-known artist and this time marries for real, though now and again Roger Diddums turns up to instruct our hero in the mysteries of the universe. When he was 75 Lucas wrote *Hetty*

Richard Cockle Lucas.

Lottie, and the Proceedings of Little Dick, in his Sky Parlour at the Tower of the Winds, the house he designed and built for himself near the Clump Inn at Chilworth (there's no point in looking for it—later renamed Chilworth Court, it was demolished in the Fifties and houses now stand on the site).

Eccentric he may have been, talented he most certainly was—sufficiently so to have one of his works mistaken for a Leonardo da Vinci. The controversy arose in 1909 when the director of a Berlin museum acquired a wax bust of a girl from a Bond Street art dealer for a large sum. It was, said the Times, deplorable that this work, by da Vinci, should have been allowed to leave the country.

Charles Cooksey, a Southampton antiquarian, promptly wrote to the newspaper declaring that it wasn't a Leonardo but an 1846 bust by Richard Cockle Lucas which was based on a painting—*Flora*—attributed to the great Master or one of his pupils. This news put the cat among the pigeons. It turned out that the museum director had forked out £9,250 for a work which, after Lucas's death, was sold for a few bob! There was a happy sequel

The sculptor who "married" a fairy

to this—R. C. L. had a posthumous exhibition at the Grafton Galleries.

There were doubters, of course—even, it seems, the Kaiser himself. But the matter was effectively clinched when a "core" within the bust was found to be part of a 19th Century English bed quilt . . .

David Lloyd in *The Buildings of England: Hampshire and the Isle of Wight* (Penguin, 1967) says of Lucas: "Not much sculptural work by him seems to survive but what there is, is good." The man who was friendly with such notables as Lord Palmerston over at Broadlands has, however, left that great West Park work which remains a memorial both to Isaac Watts and himself: the eight foot statue in grey marble, with its pedestal panels depicting Watts as a young poet, a teacher and a philospher.

The statue itself has rightly won acclaim for its lack of that pomposity often found in memorial figures. Watts has his arms outstretched and (nice touch) some jacket button undone—"realistic and convincing," says Lloyd. The statue, paid for by public subscription, was "inaugurated" by the Earl of Shaftesbury on July 17, 1861.

Over at North Stoneham Church there is a tablet to local landowner John Fleming (1844), with a portrait in relief in a sunk oval, and at Lucas's own parish church in Chilworth can be found a self-executed marble medallion with a profile of the sculptor, carved in 1840.

Lucas produced his own lengthy epitaph, listing his major works, all of which he photographed, and concluding that, "having lived to overcome all his enemies, either with high courage or gentle forbearance, and knowing Birth is a pain,

Life a labour and Eternity the reward, for which Death is a necessity, he endeavours to live for Truth that he may aspire to Death."

R. C. Lucas also wrote an epitaph for his wife Eliza, describing her as "industrious, frugal, fond and faithful." Their son, Albert Lucas (1828-1919), whose second name was that of the engraver Durer, was also an artist—he helped his father make the *Flora* bust—and is represented by a number of oil paintings in the collection of Southampton Art Gallery.

His West Park statue of Isaac Watts.

Lord Maybray-King

Horace King had a serious face and took politics seriously. He fought grimly for the underdog as a Southampton MP and later, as the Speaker, frowned his schoolmasterly disaproval of unruly elements in the House he controlled so well. The skills he had practised for many years at Taunton's School stood him in good stead in Parliament.

But there were several other lighter sides to the man: Horace the concert party pianist and accordionist; Horace the dancer sweeping the ladies off their feet; Horace the bon viveur. Not long after his ennoblement he told a reporter: "When I was a schoolteacher I was the happiest in the world, then I was the happiest Member of Parliament, now I'm the happiest Lord."

His was a Dick Whittington type of tale. Born on tough Teeside, where he was taught at a cane-dominated village school and where his parents had to watch the pennies to give him sixpenny piano lessons, Horace King fought financial hardship to finish his studies at King's College, London, playing the piano in a dance band and taking weekend private teaching work to keep going. Worst of all, he was forced to live in a tent on a common, existing on scraps of food bought cheaply from the markets. It was a way of life which gave him a duodenal ulcer and, later, months in hospital.

It has been said that Horace came to Southampton on the toss of a coin. But whether or not the young teacher intended to stay in Southampton, when he got a job at Taunton's, stay he did. "Doc" King, to whose BA had been added a Doctorate, was for 17 years head of English at the grammar school before briefly becoming head-master of Regent's Park Secondary Boys School after the war.

Local politics absorbed Horace and his wife Victoria ("Queenie"), a long-serving Labour councillor who would become Southampton's Mayor. Though his indifferent health kept him out of the Forces, Horace had a busy war in an understaffed school but still found time to entertain Service men and women on lonely sites or war workers during a midnight break. Those who enjoyed it have never forgotten his V (for victory) Concert Party, with Horace "tickling the ivories" and singing ribald and unschoolmasterly ditties like *Salome* ("Every little wiggle makes the boys all stare").

Keen to enter Parliament, Horace was adopted as Labour candidate for the New Forest in the 1945 General Election. A lost cause, of course, but invaluable experience for the battles to come. Kicks there were, too. Though Horace had appealed for a clean fight, he had to put up with

Two former pupils meet up with the "Doc" in Malawi.

66

The poor boy who became Mr. Speaker

snide Tory allusions that he fought a war out of uniform.

In course of time Horace became Labour MP for both Southampton Constituencies, Test and Itchen, and lived to see one of his old Taunton pupils, Bob Mitchell, become a local Member, too. For six of his 20 years as a Southampton MP he was Speaker of the House of Commons—Labour's first—and once confessed to feeling awe, even fear, at being faced with 600 MPs, all eager to have their say.

His job required him to stay aloof and apart from the other MPs, and that rather rankled with this most sociable and gregarious of beings. Looking back on these days in later years, he told a reporter: "I was not allowed to eat in the dining room, or drink in the bar and couldn't be seen to show any favouritism to any person or party."

Some of his old comrades expected Horace to return to the Labour Party when his days as Mr. Speaker came to an end. Because he didn't, a councillor described him to me, unkindly, as a "Ramsay Macdonald figure"; but Horace pointed out that once you became Speaker you were non-partisan for ever. On one public occasion he put it memorably: "I have exchanged party politics for something much more important—democracy."

In any case, when he was made a life baron in 1971, he found himself almost as busy as deputy Speaker of the Lords, rising at 7am at his long-time home in Manor Farm Road, near Bitterne Park Triangle, and not getting back until late in the evening. One thing was different: the House of Lords was a quiet place by comparison with the Commons and there was no trouble keeping order there. The standard of debating was better, too.

37 Manor Farm Road, Bitterne Park, Horace King's long-time home.

Being surrounded by well-heeled peers of the realm was a far cry from those far-off days in the North-East when Horace had to pawn his Sunday-best clothes because his lay preaching steel worker father was out of work; hard times when children went barefoot in summer to save their boots for colder weather.

Horace was married four times. After "Queenie's" death he remarried and was widowed a second time. A third marriage sadly ended in divorce when His Lordship was 84. Five months later he wed his long-time friend Sheila Atkinson who had nursed him through illness. But their happiness was short-lived, for in September, 1986, Horace Maybray-King—the hyphen came with the baronetcy, there already being a Lord King—died at the age of 85.

R. J. Mitchell

The story of Reginald Joseph Mitchell is so inspiring — and such a sad one, too — that its appeal to that great romantic star Leslie Howard was understandable. Actor-director Howard saw his 1942 film *The First of the Few* as a wartime propaganda vehicle and the role of Mitchell as another opportunity to play one of those absent-minded dreamers that were his speciality.

According to Dr Gordon Mitchell, editor and part-author of *R. J. Mitchell* (Nelson and Saunders, 1986), his father, though blond and blue-eyed like Howard, was temperamentally the complete opposite: "forceful, strong, quick-tempered and very much awake all the time." Ironically, neither Mitchell, whose Spitfire helped to win the Battle of Britain, nor Howard, who played him, lived to see the Nazis defeated — R. J. died of cancer in 1937 at the tragically early age of 42 and Howard was never heard of again when his plane went missing in 1943.

Reg Mitchell was born in 1895 at Stoke-on-Trent (where there's a Spitfire museum as well as a school named after him) and began life as a locomotive engineering apprentice. But he was always mad about aircraft and in 1917 became personal assistant to Hubert Scott-Paine at the Supermarine Aviation works in Woolston, Southampton. Two years later he was chief designer.

Mitchell's boss was obsessed with winning the Schneider Trophy, an international award presented to the nation having the fastest seaplane over a measured course, and in 1922 Supermarine successfully challenged the Italians with Sea Lion II, Mitchell's redesign of the firm's 1919 entry. Southampton's citizenry turned out in Cup Final style to celebrate and the old Floating Bridge was

R. J. Mitchell (seated, centre) after the Spitfire's first flight on March 5, 1936. Also in the picture (left to right): "Mutt" Summers, Vickers' chief test pilot; Mitchell's assistant, Major H. J. Payn; Stuart Scott-Hall, Air Ministry resident technical officer; and test pilot Jeffrey Quill. Photo: Southern Newspapers.

decked with flags as it carried the trophy over the water to the victor factory.

The 1923 competition saw the Americans beating Supermarine's entry Sea Lion III. Though the result was a setback for Mitchell, by the following year he had signed a ten-year contract as the company's chief designer and engineer, heralding a period which was to see many triumphs. In the 20 years of his life with Supermarine, the man his test pilots called "Mitch" designed a grand total of 24 aircraft — flying boats, amphibians, light planes and racing seaplanes, the Spitfire and a bomber he was working on when he died.

Mitchell's Schneider ambitions with his streamlined monoplane the S.4 were dashed when the seaplane met with an accident during its trials, but in the 1927 contest — Britain dropped out in 1926 — he proved triumphant by regaining the

The Spitfire designer who died at 42

trophy for Britain with the S.5 at Venice. Back home there were more celebrations, though characteristically the modest Mitchell disclaimed an individual victory: he always regarded himself as the leader of a team.

In 1929 Supermarine, which had been taken over by Vickers, entered their S.6 in the contest (now held every other year). September 7 was a beautiful day for the race — cars jammed the roads and the Solent was alive with boats of all types for what turned out be be another British win. Since the S.6 had a Rolls Royce engine it was unsurprising that the firm should provide R. J. Mitchell with one of their cars in appreciation of his genius. By now he was looking up in the world, with a nice house, built to his own design, in Russell Place at Highfield.

The Schneider Trophy races undoubtedly cheered people up in a time of economic gloom, but in 1931 the Labour Government was reluctant to fork out for his kind of entertainment. Luckily an anti-socialist millionairess, Lady Houston, was prepared to put up £100,000 and thus embarrass poor old Ramsay MacDonald. On this occasion, with the S.6B, Britain won the Trophy outright — which meant for all time.

These were the Depression years, but Supermarine, with its Schneider successes behind it and a continuing production of marine aircraft, increased the Woolston factory staff at a time when other firms were decreasing theirs. Mitchell was working on what would be his greatest creation, the Spitfire, when something appalling happened: the designer was taken seriously ill and had a major operation for cancer. This was in the summer of 1933, yet "Mitch" carried on valiantly —

less than a year after his operation he obtained his pilot's licence.

Early in 1936 the prototype Spitfire was ready to be tested. R. J.'s chairman Sir Robert McLean thought up the name, though the designer is said to have described it as "bloody silly"! The fighter flew for the first time on March 5, 1936, taking off from Eastleigh Airport. The Echo enthused: "Even the uninitiated have realised when watching the streamlined monoplane flash across the sky at five miles a minute (300 mph) that here is a plane out of the ordinary."

Leslie Howard as the dying Mitchell in the heavily romanticised 1942 film The First of the Few. *David Niven is seen as "Crisp", a fictionalised amalgam of several test pilots.*

The sad irony is that Mitchell, who died the following year, didn't live to see his creation, the most famous of all fighter planes, play its vital role in saving his country from Nazi domination. Almost 23,000 Spitfires and Seafires were built — a remarkable figure.

Mitchell's brilliance, not always fully recognised during his lifetime, has been admirably acknowledged in both his native town and adopted city since his death. A youth centre, a museum, scholarships, schools and lectures, a road, an office block and a development of flats have all been named after him.

Ivor Montagu

Ivor Montagu and his bride "Hell".
Photo: Lawrence and Wishart.

A man of many parts—that was the Hon. Ivor Montagu, and his activities represented something of a dilemma for him. In his autobiography he put it this way: "To zoologists I have been a film man, to the film world a politician, to politicians a sports specialist."

Born in 1905, the man who would later become the first film critic of both the *Observer* and the *New Statesman*, and later still Hitchcock's co-producer, was the first president of the Saints Supporters' Club at 16 and chairman and president of the Table Tennis Association before his 18th birthday—he helped to revive "Ping Pong" as a national sport. And in a remarkably varied career he not only assisted Russian film director Serge Eisenstein during the great man's brief and abortive Hollywood period but in a zoological capacity brought a wolf cub back from Yugoslavia and a bear cub back from Russia!

Most of his growing-up was centred on the Big House at Townhill Park, the seat of his banker father Lord Swaythling, and he always regarded himself as a Hampshire man and a Sotonian. He wore the county cricket tie and Saints' ties, scarves and rosettes . . . at soccer matches he used a rattle as well as a megaphone, which he admitted came in handy during his time as a silent day film director.

Grandpa, who lived at South Stoneham House in Swaythling (it's now a University hall of residence), was the second Jewish peer in Britain (Rothschild was the first). When, on his ennoblement, he asked Lord Montagu of Beaulieu whether he would mind sharing his surname with him and got the reply "I have no objection to sharing my name with you, if you will share your money with me," the new baron fell back on the name Swaythling—he'd call his heir "St. Denys" when he was in a cheerful mood!

Ivor was very fond of Townhill Park House ("big and white, inside and out") and could not bring himself to return when his eldest brother Stuart, who had succeeded to the title, eventually sold up. In his book *The Youngest Son* (Lawrence and Wishart, 1970) he writes: "I could not tell you even now what became of the house, for I have never asked" (it now belongs to the Southampton Institute of Higher Education).

After leaving Cambridge in the mid-Twenties, and before his 21st birthday, the young Montagu helped to found the Film Society, with the aim of showing good pictures unshown commercially; then came an expedition to the USSR, in search of a rare breed of vole, which preceded two important developments—he entered the film industry and he met his wife Eileen Hellstern (always knows as "Hell").

The Communist son of Lord Swaythling

Over lunch at the Cafe Royal Michael Balcon hired Ivor, at a £60 fee, to see what could be done to improve *The Lodger* (1926), the work of a young director named Alfred Hitchcock . . . with whom he got on so well that they worked together several times during the Thirties. Ivor was associate producer on *The Man Who Knew Too Much* (1934) and *The Thirty Nine Steps* (1935) and co-producer on *The Secret Agent* (1936).

He translated from the Russian Pudovkin's *Film Technique* as well as Eisenstein's collection of lectures *Film Form* and became the latter's companion and associate on his trips to Berlin, Paris, London and Hollywood—their sad adventures in Tinsel Town are chronicled in Ivor's book *With Eisenstein in Hollywood*.

Of the 26 grandchildren of Ivor's four grandparents, five, including himself, became Communists. In 1938 he went to Spain to make propaganda films for the Republicans in the Civil War and on his return issued a compilation film of the conflict called *Peace and Plenty* (1939). The Second World War found him making films for the Ministry of Information. Then he joined Ealing Studios where, among other assignments, he co-wrote *Scott of the Antarctic* (1948).

All the while Ivor continued to follow cricket and football, play chess, write political and other books, and of course remain active in table tennis, becoming referee of both English and world championships, serving countless times as captain of England and finally retiring at 63 as founder-president of the International Table Tennis Federation.

1959 was a big year for Ivor—he was awarded the coveted Lenin Peace Prize. Six years later came his book about film appreciation, *Film World*. He continued to be active into his old age, writing his autobiography and pieces for film magazines. His last article for *Sight and Sound*, journal of the British Film Institute, was in 1984—a review of a book about his old mentor Eisenstein. Said editor Penelope Houston: "As usual his copy was written in a minute and none too immediately legible hand on numerous small sheets of paper torn from a note pad. The deciphering of Ivor's contributions was something of an art in itself; more satisfying than the delivery of some immaculately typed manuscripts."

By Guy Fawkes Day of that year, however, there came an end to the voice that could discourse with equal authority on small mammals, world cinema or the Communist Party of Gret Britain. Ivor Montagu died at 80, preceded a month earlier by his beloved "Hell."

Footnote: Ivor's second brother, the Hon. Ewen Montagu, took up the Law and rose to become Recorder of Southampton.

Townhill Park House.

Billy Reid

Billy Reid the accordionist.

Billy Reid, born on September 9, 1902, at 1 Coronation Terrace, St Mary Street, had a spectacular rise from humble beginnings. Though his declining years were clouded by bankruptcy and sadness, the songs he wrote are still sung all over the world. Especially *The Gypsy*.

Billy, who began his working life as a riveter at Southampton Docks, was the second son of a wharfinger, George Reid, and his wife Florence Mary, who lived in the now vanished Princess Street in Chapel. Though they weren't musicians themselves, their children were given sixpenny music lessons, a debt they handsomely repaid.

There were five boys and two girls: George played the sax, Billy the piano (he took up accordion later), Albert the organ, Florrie the piano, Johnny the piano and accordion, and Win the organ. The only non-instrumental sibling was "Nobby", though he made up for the deficiency by unswerving fraternal loyalty.

As youngsters in the Twenties, George and Billy had their own band, which began life at Trinity Hall, Kingsland — George hired the premises and "Nobby" took the money on the door. The Ariste Dance Orchestra won a considerable degree of local fame before George and Billy went professional and left to play for afternoon tea dances in Glasgow and Edinburgh.

In a sense it was a kind of homecoming, for the Reid family had Scottish blood — great-grandfather Reid, a doctor of music, was a Scot. The Reid band certainly proved popular — on one occasion, at the Marine Gardens, Portobello, they played for 4,000 dancers! Billy and George stayed 11 years.

After a spell in Maurice Winnick's band at Selfridge's, Billy heard that Noel Coward needed an accordionist for his operetta *Bitter-Sweet*. At that time Billy didn't play the accordion, so he hired one, went home to practise, passed the audition and remained in the show for two years. It was this experience that prompted him to form his famous accordion band which toured the variety theatres of the Thirties — and in particular attracted full houses at his home-town theatre, the Hippodrome in Ogle Road.

The band — George was in it, too — came to an end with the outbreak of war.

In the Forties Billy Reid began his prolific songwriting career, turning out — with apparent ease — hit after hit for his partner, the singer

The dockland riveter who became a famous songwriter

Dorothy Squires, with whom he topped the bill at the London Palladium.

Like Irving Berlin and Cole Porter he was equally adept with lyrics and music and was often called the fastest writer in the business. The legend went that he wrote *The Gypsy,* which sold millions of records, in three minutes, and another hit, *The Tree in the Meadow,* in five!

As dollar earners in the post-war Forties Billy and Dorothy were considered two of Chancellor Stafford Cripps' best friends. Success after success came from the Reid pen: Louis Armstrong and the Inkspots sold seven million discs with *The Gypsy,* Ella Fitzgerald had a hit with *It's a Pity to Say Goodnight,* Frank Sinatra and Dinah Shore scored with *I'll Close My Eyes,* Eddie Fisher's version of *I'm Walking Behind You* was 22 weeks in the charts. *Coming Home* proved a poignant after-the-war success and at one time *I Still Believe* and *Bridge of Sighs* seemed hardly ever off the air.

At the height of his fame, in the late Forties, Billy was reputed to be earning up to £1,000 a week. But everything seemed to go tragically awry. In 1958, when he agreed to be judged bankrupt, his assets were stated to be only £56 — £6 in cash, and a fridge and a piano worth £50. So what had gone wrong?

It seems he put money into companies that lost heavily over the years. In order to continue to run a song publishing concern, a theatrical agency and a theatre in Wales, he claimed he'd had to sell his car and personal effects to pay wages. And there had been a legal dispute over a house.

Billy Reid continued to play the piano on the Isle of Wight, where he made his home. Throughout the years of their brother's success George and Johnny ran bands in Southampton — George at one time had the residency at the Polygon Hotel. George, too, lives on the Island now, still hale and hearty at 88, and Johnny, not in such good health, recently moved from Woolston to Ferndown.

Youngest sister Win sings, dances and plays the organ in the Southampton East Point Follies which entertains senior citizens, and over on the Isle of Wight the Reid musical tradition carries on through Billy's widow Jane — singer Janet Gordon — and their son Billy Junior.

Billy (30), who fronts his own band has written an incredible 9,000 songs — which would have delighted his prolific father. But Billy Junior hasn't forgotten the songs of Billy Senior, who died 14 years ago at the age of 71. This chip-off-the-old-block has put *The Gypsy* on tape, with his mother as the vocalist. . . .

February, 1947: Billy and Dorothy Squires sail for America in the Queen Elizabeth.

73

Stanley Ridges

Stanley Charles Ridges was a familiar face in Hollywood films between 1934 and 1951 (when he died). He specialised in lawyers, doctors, professors, business men and, on occasion, crooks. But his career, which began in church hall concert parties, started off lightheartedly in song and dance. And off-stage, too, say his surviving relatives and friends, his mien was boisterous and life-loving—a far cry from the sobersides his movie portrayals suggest.

Born in 1891 at 27 Hillside Avenue in the Liberal-inspired suburb of Bitterne Park, the eldest of 11 children, Stan (as he was always known) showed an early aptitude for entertainment—he "hoofed" in a minstrel show with other members of the Ridges family and his fellow pals from Bitterne Park School. Even after joining the Merchant Navy—mainly, I suspect, so he could get to see the shows on Broadway—Stan dreamed of show business. Eventually he jumped ship to become a chorus boy.

He graduated to small parts and juvenile leads. Then came the war, which found him serving in France as a Royal Canadian Flying Corps pilot . . . but still acting in amateur theatricals behind the lines.

After the Armistice, Stan was back in Britain, keen to put his dancing shoes back on. In 1919 he joined the male chorus of a new Jerome Kern musical called *Oh Joy!* (curiously retitled from its original American *Oh, Boy!*), which opened at the Kingsway Theatre on January 27 starring the young Beatrice Lillie.

He was back on Broadway the following year in another Kern show, Florenz Ziegfeld's production of *Sally*, played by Marilyn Miller. By this time, though, the former choirboy from Bitterne Park parish church had really arrived in his chosen profession—he was fourth down the cast list and had two songs in the musical which was to make Broadway history with 570 performances.

The remainder of the Twenties found him performing in several other musicals, including the *Tea for Two* show *No, No Nanette*. But it would seem that it was the Gershwin show *Smarty* (1927), in which he was to have co-starred with Fred and Adele Astaire, which prompted him to hand in his dancing shoes and become a straight actor. After six turbulent try-out weeks, during which there were numerous changes, out came Stanley (and the song *How Long Has This Been Going On?*), the musical re-emerging as the Broadway and West End hit *Funny Face*.

In the early Thirties he established a high reputation as a member of the Theatre Guild company, touring the nation in such plays as *Mary of Scotland*. In 1934 he was to have appeared opposite the rising Katharine Hepburn in *Dark Victory* (later a Bette Davis film hit) but evidently Kate and Stan found themselves mutually incompatible and the Southampton-born actor withdrew before the provincial try-out.

From Hillside Avenue to Hollywood

The Ridges family home: 27 Hillside Avenue, Bitterne Park.

That year, however, marked the beginning of his Hollywood period (though he had made his movie debut in 1923 and appeared in a couple of 1930 shorts). Director-screenwriters Ben Hecht and Charles MacArthur liked Ridges and cast him in two of their films, *Crime Without Passion* with Claude Rains and *The Scoundrel* with Noel Coward (a sympathetic role as villainous Coward's much-put-upon romantic rival).

In 1936 he had an important part as Shadow in *Winterset*, a verse drama inspired by the Sacco and Vanzetti case (in which two anarchists were allegedly executed on trumped-up charges for political reasons). The author was Maxwell Anderson, a playwright with whose work Stanley Ridges was familiar, having played on stage in his *Valley Forge* and *Mary of Scotland* for the Theatre Guild.

Though he appeared in countless movies, character parts in which his true talents could shine were rare. In *Black Friday* (1940) he inherited from a sick Bela Lugosi the role of a mild professor into whose brain Boris Karloff puts the brain of a gangster. It was Stan's big chance and he took it, winning critical plaudits.

Other roles stood out: the kindly psychiatrist in *Possessed*, with Joan Crawford; Professor Siletsky in the Jack Benny comedy *To Be or Not To Be*; Gary Cooper's commanding officer in *Sergeant York*; and, best of all, the Scotland Yard inspector playing a cat-and-mouse game with wife murderer Charles Laughton in *The Suspect*. The Forties was the actor's best period.

Bitterne Park rarely saw Stan, but he kept in touch with his large family of brothers and sisters and returned home for his mother's funeral in 1933. In the late Thirties, his father, James, and his youngest sister, Ruby, visited Stan in America and purportedly had a wonderful time with their ebullient host. Ruby liked it so much that she later made her home in America, and lives there still.

Though he worked in Hollywood, Stanley Ridges was far fonder of Connecticut, where he had a summer home at Westbrook. There the residents of this quiet spot recall the actor as an inveterate party-giver who loved a stiff drink.

Stanley Ridges in his best screen role: as the transformed professor in Black Friday.   *Photo: Universal Pictures.*

He died at 57, having completed a thankless role in a dim Ginger Rogers comedy called *The Groom Wore Spurs*, leaving an American wife, Dorothy, but no children, though he had a step-daughter always known as "Sugar". He was, however, uncle to a huge Ridges clan back in Southampton where most of his brothers and sisters had remained. Several brothers worked for the Ordnance Survey, like their father; others went into teaching, the Post Office and shop management.

General Juan de Rosas

Not many people of distinction, disembarking at Southampton, have decided to settle in the seaport. But for General Juan Manuel de Rosas, of course, there was no going back: the dictator of Argentina, allegedly responsible for putting 15,000 people to death, had fled for his life after one of those regular coups with which South America has always been familiar.

The year was 1852. The general's army had been defeated in February at the battle of Monte Caseros. After 15 years the Argentinians had had enough of him and rallied to another general, Justpo Urquiza, who — with Brazilian and Uruguayan support — managed to get Rosas on the run. In 1861 the Argentine Congress condemned him to die in his absence as a mass murderer.

By then he was safely in Rockstone House, Carlton Crescent. But why did Rosas, who was to stay in Southampton for a quarter of a century, choose the Hampshire town as his place of exile?: Captain Day, skipper of the warship HMS Centaur which brought Rosas, his wife and daughter to our shores, was a native of Southampton and perhaps was able to convince the general that no more suitable haven could be found. Doubtless Rosas dreamed of taking a return boat to Montevideo from his adopted port.

He was broke when he got here, but in due course £100,000 came through from Buenos Aires, proceeds from the sale of his cattle. After about 13 years in his stylish Regency terrace house the former dictator turned farmer, renting the 400-acre Burgess Street Farm at Swaythling from squire Fleming of Stoneham Park. By now the general was a familiar, striking figure in South-ampton, riding through the streets on a beautiful black horse and behaving with all the imperiousness and hauteur that had characterised his years as boss of the Argentine.

He treated his farm workers as if they were peons, hiring them by the hour and not allowing them to speak to him except in answer to questions or in acknowledging commands — though in fairness he paid "over the odds" in wages. But the man once dubbed "Blood Red Rosas" could, apparently, be thoughtful. In his first year in Southampton he presented his Bernard Street hairdresser with a silver shaving basin.

Though Rosas, born in 1793 and 84 when he died in 1877, had a bloodthirsty reputation, some apologists have held that the general was less responsible for the atrocities than two secret

Rockstone House, 8 Carlton Crescent, once the home of General Rosas.   *Photo: Wendy Stott.*

Exiled dictator on a black horse

General Rosas.

are forgotten in the light of his significance as a national unifier.

General Rosas is buried in Southampton's Old Cemetery beside his daughter Manuela, her husband and their son. Supporters of the general — his political heirs are the Peronists — had the memorial renovated in 1965. It was, of course, inevitable that there should be a request for his remains to be returned to Argentina and it finally came in 1974. But following a change of Government this Peronist project was abandoned.

Juan de Rosas had his first whiff of battle in the streets of Buenos Aires at the age of 14 during a conflict which finally threw out an expeditionary force from, ironically, his future home, Britain. As a young man he set up his country's first meat salting plant, but — embittered by restrictive laws affecting his business — later took up politics.

This was a time when Argentina was a bubbling cauldron of near-permanent civil war. Rosas raised a cowboy army and, in the 1820s, at the head of 600 horsemen, took over Buenos Aires. From 1835 he was dictator of the entire land.

When Montevideo became filled with anti-Rosas refugees, the general decided "to intervene in the affairs of Uruguay." That country lapsed into civil war, one side taking the side of Rosas. But the Argentinian seige of Montevideo failed, the defenders — among whom was Garibaldi — stubbornly succeeded.

Soon the general found himself at war with Chile, Brazil, Peru, Paraguay. In 1852 he was defeated at the battle of Monte Caseros and went into exile. Life in faraway Southampton must have seemed humdrum after such a violent and exciting career.

societies, one derived from the mob and the other from the elite, which bolstered his regime. But certainly it's true that this son of a wealthy ranch-owner governed his country with great severity from 1835 until 1852.

At first he ruled moderately. Things changed for the worse when an uprising by political enemies took place. Government forces slaughtered the rebels and severely punished their supporters. The rebel colour, blue, was virtually outlawed. Red was everywhere — red sashes and red shawls predominated. But life in an oppressive country which even banned migration soon became unbearable.

Yet many Argentinians look upon Rosas, for all his horrors (torture, aggression against neighbours, secret police, faked elections) as one of their great founding fathers, comparable in Latin American terms to Washington or Franklin. His wars against the Indians and the Uruguayans

Ken Russell

Just after the war Southampton-born film director Ken Russell, trying to get into the film industry rather than take a job in the family boot and shoe business, was so entranced by a performance of the Tchaikovsky piano concerto that he rushed into a Portswood shop, Godfrey's, to buy it.

In those days the record department was managed by a chap called Dennis Wheeler, who died in 1988. Russell never forgot how sympathetic and understanding Wheeler had been. He told his biographer: "He saw my basic enthusiasm and gradually led me from the realms of romantic Tchaikovsky to the shattering world of Stravinsky. He'd say 'Buy this' or 'Listen to this'."

Whether admirers of Tchaikovsky will remain equally grateful to Wheeler after Russell's screen biography of the composer — the controversial 1970 *The Music Lovers* — is another matter: Stravinsky remains untackled by Southampton's ageing *enfant terrible*.

Russell, wrote Leslie Halliwell, sets out to shock people and has done so with flair but no subtlety. But the extravagances of biographical films like *Mahler* (1974) and the television-made *Dance of the Seven Veils* (1970), about Richard Strauss, can be set against the touching, unforgettable Delius study *Song of Summer,* produced for TV in 1968, or the restrained portrait of sculptor Gaudier-Brzeska *Savage Messiah* (1972). One thing is certain: Russell's vivid pictorial imagination ensures that the viewer is never bored — shocked, perhaps, or irritated, even angered. But nobody falls asleep.

Ken Russell was born in 1928 into a footwear family which, until comparatively recent years, when their business came under new manage-

Ken Russell on the set of his film Valentino *(1977). Photo: Barry Peake; United Artists Corporation.*

ment, had a branch in Eastleigh as well as others in Shirley Road and St Mary Street. But he chose not to follow in father Henry's shoesteps. When he was at Taunton's School the young Russell was laying the foundations for a showbiz career.

He produced wartime shows and concerts and continued putting them on at Pangbourne Nautical College and in the RAF during his National Service. Later he became a rep actor, a ballet dancer and a photographer for Picture Post. And he cut his cinematic eye teeth on some striking amateur films.

Though Ken was always close to his family, his parents didn't see much of him when he was a young man. "He was always such a roamer," said Ethel, his mother and biggest fan. Those roamings led to the BBC, where he had attracted the attention of Huw Wheldon, boss of the Monitor arts programme (on which another Sotonian, theatre director Patrick Garland, also worked). His film on Elgar, made in 1962 for the programme's

"Success in art is 90 per cent drudgery"

hundredth edition, won the Screen Writers' Guild Award for the best documentary of that year.

Ken Russell is always being accused, with some justification, of vulgarity and tastelessness — one commentator remarked, after seeing his outrageous *Lisztomania* (1975), that if it had been Russell's first film he would never have worked again. Films like *The Devils* (1971) and *Crimes of Passion* (1984) have sequences some believe cross the boundary from the lurid into the pornographic.

But his 1969 D. H. Lawrence adaptation, *Women in Love,* was well received and *The Boy Friend* (1971) struck most of the few who saw it as a charming period musical, though neither the director nor its composer enjoyed the experience. For Sandy Wilson, his long-running small-scale show had turned into "a Walpurgisnacht of self-indulgence." Russell's extravagant, over-the-top style was, however, admirably suited to the rock musical *Tommy* (1974), which remains one of his best films (the management of the Odeon gave Ken's late mother Ethel, a familiar face in the cinema's much-mourned cafe, a ticket a day for its entire run).

The ogre many of his movies suggest — the man who, on live television, could strike a film critic over the head with a rolled-up copy of his newspaper — seems a far cry from the quiet man his friends and family know or the reflective one journalist Jasmine Profit encountered in 1972 on location in Dorset for *Savage Messiah*.

The film illustrated that everyone had the ability to be an artist, he told her: "they can develop, use and exploit it — it's just a question of recognising it. A lot of people get side-tracked on the way

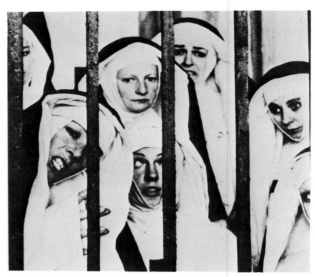

The frenzied nuns of Ken Russell's controversial 1971 film The Devils. Photo: Russo Productions/Warner Bros.

and disillusioned and discouraged." Success in art, he added, was 90 per cent drudgery, nine per cent luck and one per cent inspiration.

Certainly Ken Russell has always been a workaholic. He is the only British film director ever to have had three films playing first-run London engagements simultaneously. He remains as busy as ever, directing operas on stage, making characteristically lively films and occasionally coming down from his Lade District hideaway, like a bandit from the hills, to make a foray into the medium that made his name (a good example was his provocative ABC of British music a year or two back).

One dream project revealed in a Seventies interview remains unfulfilled. This would have been a television look at the Southampton and Hampshire of his Thirties childhood. A pity it never happened. Maybe some day it will.

William Shayer

These days the paintings of William Shayer fetch huge sums, yet this popular recorder of the Victorian rural scene had a hard time of it during much of his lifetime. In 1792, when he was five years old, his publican father died, leaving his mother to run the Horse and Jockey in East Street, Southampton, and bring up the family on her own.

Shayer found himself in a similar position when, in 1823, his first wife Sarah died, leaving him with five children. At this time he was still struggling to establish himself as a landscape painter. The Hampshire Herald recognised his difficulties a few years later in an enthusiastic review of his exhibited work: "We fully understand how great the struggle must have been to him to raise to the heights he has done in art with a numerous family to bring up, and his perseverance does him honour."

His beginnings were certainly humble enough. Admittedly he started as a painter . . . but as a painter of rush button chairs! He progressed to coach painting, a trade in which many other well-known artists began — people like John Martin and Peter Monamy who, like Shayer, are represented in the collection at Southampton Art Gallery. As Brian Stewart and Mervyn Cutten, exhaustive researchers of William Shayer's life, have underlined, coach painting provided a thorough technical grounding which stood artists in good stead in their later careers.

At Chichester in 1810 Shayer worked for a master coach builder named George Parsons and married his niece Sarah Earle somewhat hurriedly in September of that year. Seven months later came the birth of their son, William Joseph, who was to

follow his father's profession, though specialising in coaching and sporting subjects rather than the rustic scene.

Another suggestion of hard times was William Shayer's 1815 conviction for poaching, though things began to look up a little in 1819 when he was commissioned to paint the funeral hatchment for the fourth Duke of Rutland. A year later he was exhibiting for the first time at the Royal Academy. By 1821 Shayer had returned to his native Southampton, taking up residence next door to the theatre in French Street.

In those far-off days long before the grants, artists sought out wealthy patrons. Shayer found one in a self-made man named Michael Hoy who owned estates not only at Thornhill and Midanbury but in the Isle of Wight. Hoy, who died in 1828, is said to have filled rooms at one of his houses with Shayer's work.

A painter's triumph over adversity

Wash Day Companions, a Shayer painting in a private collection.
(Photo: Richard Green Galleries, London.)

1823 saw the deaths not only of Shayer's mother but of his wife Sarah. Not long after he married another publican's daughter — pubs seemed to figure largely in his family history! Wife No 2 was Elizabeth Waller of the Duke's Head in Purtney (Sarah's father had been mine host of Chichester's Anchor Inn). This union produced two more painters-to-be — Charles, who became quite well-known, and Henry.

By now William's fortunes had improved. The opening of Henry Buchan's Hampshire Picture Gallery at 159 High Street certainly helped. Unsurprisingly, in view of a popularity that has persisted, buyers even then sought out the Shayers. In 1828 the painter took up residence at No 158, next door to the gallery, then moved to nearby Hanover Buildings in 1823, finally winding up — after a spell in Nursling — at Bladon Lodge, Shirley, in 1843. He was still there when he died, 36 years later, at the great age of 92.

His declining years, however, were blighted by illness and in particular by blindness — he painted his last work in 1870. He died on December 21, 1879, and is buried in the churchyard at the parish church of St. James in Shirley.

It is easy to understand enthusiasm for this artist. Shayer's work doesn't just appeal to collectors — his paintings can often be seen on greeting cards and calendars.

The landscape he loved was that of the New Forest and his canvasses depict with immense charm and great technical skill its copses, cattle, horses and Gypsy encampments. Shayer gives us as attractive a picture of rural life in Victorian England as one could imagine — idealised perhaps, but then he sought to convey beauty rather than social realism. He was prolific, too, eventually achieving a total of 426 paintings at London galleries.

Two years ago saw his bicentenary celebrated at Southampton with an Esso-sponsored exhibition of some of his finest paintings, with loans from the Tate Gallery, the Fitzwilliam Museum at Cambridge and the Guildhall Art Gallery.

Not bad for a humble lad from Lower East Street.

John Stonehouse

Back in 1968, when John Stonehouse was at the apex of his political career in the role of Postmaster General, the first son of a Post Office worker to achieve such heights, my late colleague Gordon Sewell went off to London to interview him for the Southern Evening Echo. He didn't enjoy the experience: Stonehouse, he told me, lacked warmth.

In the light of later developments in the Southampton-born politician's life, Gordon's article makes interesting reading. He wrote: "The youthful-looking 43-year-old Minister — tall, handsome and impeccably dressed — gives rather the impression of a Big Business tycoon who is just about to conclude a multi-million deal."

Yet Stonehouse, born into a Socialist family in 1925, was nurtured on that idealism which burned so brightly in the souls of the young during and after the war. Something went badly wrong as well as triumphantly right in a life which was to end so ignobly with his faked disappearance in Miami and his imprisonment for theft and false pretences.

The son of William, PO engineer and dedicated trade union official, and Rosina, the formidable Labour councillor who later became Mayor of her son's native city, won a Taunton's School scholarship from Springhill, the Catholic primary school opposite the Dell. At the grammar school his English master was Dr Horace King, later a Southampton MP, the first Labour Speaker and finally Lord Maybray-King.

"Doc," Stonehouse confessed, wasn't impressed with him. The boy, 16 at the time, had limited ability in his teacher's view and should be apprenticed to a butcher! Did this remark act as a spur for

John Stonehouse the post-debacle novelist. Echo photo.

the man who in years to come would have ambitions to become Prime Minister? Butchery was abandoned in favour of the Southampton Probation Service: his job as a clerk-typist there strengthened his belief in that need for social change already ingrained in him by his family background.

Between 1944 and 1947 he was in the RAF and after demob studied at the London School of

The politician who came back from the dead

Economics, graduating with honours. His contact with African students at LSE gave him a lifelong interest in the continent and he spent two years in Uganda setting up co-operatives. By now Stonehouse was really on his way and in 1957 was elected MP for Wednesbury.

In that first year he hit the headlines when he was expelled from the abortive Central African Federation, an episode which prompted his book *Prohibited Immigrant* — the title refers to the Kenyan colonial government's reaction to Stonehouse's earlier defence of Mau-Mau suspects he had believed to be innocent. Idealism at this stage in his life was still paramount.

With Labour in power again in 1964 Stonehouse's rise was rapid: Parliamentary Secretary to the Ministry of Aviation in that year; Under Secretary of State for the Colonies in 1966; Minister of State at the Department of Technology in 1967; and Postmaster General in 1968. Gordon Sewell described the Stonehouse of that year as a "businessman-politician" — an appropriate description for the president of the London Co-operatiave Society, one of the country's largest retail organisations.

Perhaps it was not so surprising that, with Labour in Opposition, Stonehouse should turn his attention to becoming something of the Big Business tycoon he already resembled in the eyes of observers like Gordon Sewell. John Stonehouse was soon controlling an empire of 20 closely-knit companies.

In due course there was considerable adverse comment on his business methods and there were rumours of financial difficulties. The rumours were true: those difficulties led to that world-

John Stonehouse the post-war Labour candidate. The election leaflet reveals that he was still at the LSE when he stood for Twickenham.

documented Florida vanishing act — he'd said he was going for a swim. But his carefully prepared plot to fake his death and to assume the identity of another man failed when he was arrested in Australia and extradited. A seven-year prison sentence ended a career that had begun so promisingly.

Released, the disgraced politician never gave up defending himself, claiming experts had diagnosed that his was a genuine case of "psychiatric suicide." Few were impressed or even sympathetic, though many admired his gritty determination in the face of adversity. He had a serious heart attack while in jail and his health wasn't good but he continued to show that life was for living.

He began a second career, as a novelist, married his mistress and former secretary Sheila Buckley and began a new life with a new family not far from his roots — in the Forest-hugging estate of new housing at Calmore. And it was there that John Thompson Stonehouse — idealist, deceiver and introducer of the infamous two-tier postal system — died on April 4, 1988.

General Shrapnel

General Henry Shrapnel, whose surname passed into the language, failed to obtain the riches and recognition he thought, correctly, that he deserved. He had his admirers but somehow appropriate rewards eluded him. Bad luck seems to have played its part.

The Duke of Wellington, you'd be right in assuming, was a powerful ally to have. Though he thought highly of the soldier-inventor's first experimental shells, the Iron Duke felt that their proven success in battle would have to be kept from the public. As Shrapnel would thus be deprived of fame and honour, Wellington believed his reward should be ample.

It wasn't. The bad luck continued years later, in 1837, when he was the guest of William IV at Brighton. The monarch personally acknowledged the country's indebtedness to the general whose invention had cost him thousands from his own purse and whose shells were said to have helped turn the tide at Waterloo. On April 23 came a letter from Windsor Castle intimating that a Baronetcy would be conferred. But, alas, the Sailor King died shortly afterwards and nothing was done.

Shrapnel, who died at Pear Tree House, Southampton, in 1842, was born at Bradford-on-Avon in Wiltshire in 1761. His early inventiveness was shown while serving as an artillery officer at the 1793 retreat from Dunkirk when he came up with two neat ideas. One was for blocking the wheels of gun carriages so that they could be skidded over the sands; another was the lighting of decoy fires to fool the enemy.

Arrowsmith's portrait of General Shrapnel. Photo: Royal Artillery Institution, Woolwich.

Though Shrapnel devoted himself to military inventions from his earliest days in the Army, spending his own money freely to develop them, he concentrated most of his attention on the shell which bears his name and which was recommended for use by the Army Board of Ordnance as

The inventor who died a disappointed man

early as 1803. Manufacture was carried out at a Scottish ironworks.

The Duke of Wellington took it up for use in the Peninsular War, the commander of the artillery writing to the Duke: "The shell is admirable to the whole army and its effects dreadful." Then came Waterloo and more praise, this time from Sir George Wood, commander of the brigade of artillery.

From Waterloo village Sir George wrote to Shrapnel on June 21, 1815, that it was doubtful whether any effort of the British could have recovered the farmhouse of La Haye Sainte without the shell. It turned the tide.

Though Henry Shrapnel was promoted to colonel in 1813 and regimental colonel a year later, practical recompense and recognition for his invention remained unforthcoming. The Board of Ordnance told him they had no funds for awards of merit. But in 1814 the Treasury granted him a pension for life of £1,200.

According to the Dictionary of National Biography, however, the terms were interpreted in such a way that Shrapnel would have been better off if it had never been awarded. Promoted to major general, he retired from active service in 1825 (though he became a colonel commandant of the Royal Artillery in 1827 and lieutenant general a decade later).

Shrapnel's first Southampton home was in Bugle Street where the new St. Michael's Vicarage now stands, but the mid-1830s found him living with his wife and daughter at the 17th Century Pear Tree House (which survives in Pear Tree Avenue as a rest home for the elderly). It was there that he died.

Perhaps because of bitterness over the disappointments of his life, Shrapnel took no part in public affairs during his quiet retirement. Though he was one of the area's more distinguished residents, he and his family seem to have avoided the social round and when he died obituaries in local papers were curiously brief.

The Hampshire Advertiser, though, did make reference to some other Shrapnel inventions, including "snuffers and corkscrews" and a "regulating pivot pen," and a gunsmith advertised "Lt. Gen. Shrapnel's patent fowling piece." But it's the "spherical case shell" for which he will always be remembered, even though Shrapnel has come to mean its bursting fragments rather than the shell itself.

The general is buried in the family vault at Holy Trinity, Bradford-on-Avon.

Pear Tree House today.

Richard Taunton

Though Richard Taunton (1684-1752) made a lot of money, some of it by privateering, he was a generous benefactor. From his wealth came the grammar school, now sixth-form college, which bears his name — though because of the contesting of his will by some of his relatives it was some years before his benefaction could be put into operation.

Alderman Taunton, twice mayor of Southampton, was a founder of the Royal Hampshire County Hospital at Winchester in 1736 and left it £5,000 in his will. The Corporation he had served got £1,400 for "pious and charitable uses" — including the relief of "decayed Aldermen" (so unlike himself) and their widows.

Twenty guineas went to the incumbent of Holy Rood Church for reading prayers twice a day: in the ruins of this blitzed church, now a memorial to the Merchant Navy, lies Taunton's tomb, moved there in 1958 from its original site in St John's churchyard. And up at Weyhill, near Andover, where Taunton had a house, £200 was given to provide 24 weekly loaves for the poor.

Taunton's trustees got the approval of the Court of Chancery in 1760 for a plan not only to aid the poor of St John's parish in Southampton, but also to provide education for boys with a sea career in mind — training, that is, in mathematics and navigation to fit them to become ships' officers. From this bequest came Taunton's School.

The first boys, equipped with green serge uniforms, were nominated in 1760. In the early days the seafaring stipulation wasn't insisted upon and the pupils were allowed to chose "any mechanical trade" . . . but this, too, was dropped in favour of a general education. The school, like

The portrait of the founder which hangs in the principal's office at Richard Taunton College.

its rival King Edward's, moved about a bit before settling in Highfield.

Not a great deal is known about Richard Taunton's early days. He was the son of a maltster, also christened Richard, whose sister Sarah married Isaac Watts the elder — the hymn writer, of *Our God Our Help in Ages Past* which chimes out from the Civic Centre clock, was thus the younger Richard's cousin. When the divine died in 1748 the alderman became his trustee for a bequest of £7 "to poor persons who usually worship in the Church of England." And on Richard Taunton's own death there were bequests to the Watts family.

School founder was enriched by the spoils of war

Taunton's money was mainly made by importing wine — he had some important customers, among them the Duke of Chandos. Wars, of course, tend to interrupt imports and exports, and Taunton's business was affected by the 1739 conflict with Spain and by the War of the Austrian Succession in the 1740s.

War gives as well as takes away, as many an entrepreneur before and after Taunton discovered. He was part owner of two privateers, the Prince Frederick and the Duke, which in 1745 fought three French ships from the South Seas and secured their cargo of (among other valuables) "45 wagon-loads of silver."

As the then headmaster of Taunton's, R. P. Challacombe, wrote in a 1952 Southern Evening Echo article, Taunton's large share of the booty "probably made him more ambitious." When the war ended he helped form a joint stock company, with no less a person than the Prince of Wales as its governor, with the object of gaining a herring-and-cod domination in British waters.

The College today.

The wine merchant invested £5,000 in the company — the Society of the Free British Fishery — and supervised the building of special ships called "herring busses", one of which was named *Taunton*. Meantime, as business flourished, Richard was active in the affairs of his native town, becoming a burgess in 1721, Senior Bailiff in 1723 and Sheriff in 1724. Ten years later he was Mayor, and again in 1743. By 1745 he was a JP.

Taunton, for all his beneficence could be ruthless when the occasion warranted it. Dr Horace King (later Lord Maybray-King), a long-time Taunton's master who became Southampton MP and the first Labour Speaker of the House of Commons, happened upon an incident in Parliamentary papers which illustrates this.

In 1735, during Taunton's first mayoralty, a Parliamentary committee inquired into the election of one of two Southampton MPs. Whigs and Tories had challenged voters on either side and Taunton was eager to secure the return of the sitting Tory. Those were the days, of course, when only a few people had the vote, and it seems that Taunton, as returning officer, had objected to some of these voters.

Before the House of Commons committee Taunton alleged that 18 of the Whig candidate's voters were foreigners. One he believed to be so "by his language and his looks." When he was asked how he could tell a foreigner by his looks, he replied: "They are easily known, by their fawning"!

Only those who voted for his candidate were liked by Mr Taunton. This time he lost out and Parliament decided that the Whig was the rightful MP.

Walter Taylor

Wellington said that the Battle of Waterloo was won on the playing fields of Eton. Could it be that the Battle of Trafalgar was won in Westgate Street in the Southampton parish of St. Michael?

It was there that Walter Taylor (1734-1803) and his father developed what a plaque on the medieval Westgate calls "inventions of great importance to the Royal Navy between the years 1750 and 1758."

First with his father, who died in 1762, and then on his own, Walter helped to pioneer the machine tool industry, which enabled woodblocks for the Navy to be produced on a mass scale. In the Maritime Museum at Southampton is a portrait of Walter Taylor holding the circular saw he is credited with inventing and which is almost identical in form to the circular saws of recent times.

Remarkable family, the Taylors. This particular Walter was the third in a family of master carpenters. The second Walter was as inventive as his son proved to be — while a prisoner of the French at Rouen in 1746 he constructed a powerful electrical machine with an ostrich egg in the place of a glass cylinder!

While working as a ship's carpenter Walter II had become struck by the rough construction of the lifting tackle and pumps with which the sailing ships were equipped and decided to do something about it. So with his son, who had begun his working life as an apprentice blockmaker, he set out to put his new ideas on the subject into practice.

In a windowless Westgate Street cellar father and son began to develop the machinery which was to serve the Navy so well in the years to come.

Walter Taylor with the circular saw. Photo: Southampton Museums.

Not only did blocks become smaller and lighter but friction was reduced and efficiency increased.

The Taylors carried on their business in Westgate Street and Bugle Street from 1754. But with the expansion of work for the Navy, Walter III, whose father had died in 1762, moved his premises first of all to land off Weston Lane, where he built a watermill on a stream emptying to an Itchen estuary, and then to an ancient mill at

Master carpenter to the Royal Navy

South Stoneham. This, of course, was Woodmill, though not the present one (that was built after the original burnt down, around 1820).

The size of Walter's enterprise can be gauged by his needing to open other block works at Deptford and Walton-on-Thames. The works at Woodmill and elsewhere are credited with having made half a million or more blocks in the years before the Battle of Trafalgar.

Former Southampton Harbour Board Engineer J. P. M. Pannell, who researched the Taylors assiduously in the Fifties, pointed out that at Trafalgar, Taylor's blocks, guaranteed for seven years, hoisted the sails and ran out the guns without failure or delay and that his pumps cleared the ships of water with a minimum of manpower.

In the ten years from 1792 Walter Taylor received a third of a million pounds for blocks supplied to the Admiralty. But he seems to have been a caring wealthy man. At his home,

Portswood Lodge, which stood between Abbott's Way and Portswood Road, he added a schoolroom for his workers' children.

It's true to say that when he died at 69 in 1803 his work was completed. His inventions were the ancestors of today's machine tools and production techniques. In the year of his death, though, the Taylor contracts were cancelled (later they were renewed on a short-term basis). That cancellation seems to have been prompted in part by a Commission set up to inquire into Naval abuses and partly in anticipation of a scheme for the Admiralty to produce its own blocks.

Taylor's family was well provided for. Just as well, for they were left with workshops but no Government orders — a sad ending to a story which began with experiments in a dark Westgate Street cellar, carried out in such secrecy that neighbours believed Walter and his father were in league with the Devil.

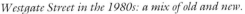

Westgate Street in the 1980s: a mix of old and new.

Captain John Treasure Jones

In historical terms the golden era of the great liners was not a lengthy one, but time was when much or most of Southampton's prosperity and fame revolved around these beloved leviathans. Though trippers coached hundreds of miles to view them, the townsfolk, with relatives toiling in their engine rooms or stewarding the "grills", tended to take the big ships for granted. Now old-timers viewing with some disdain the "yuppie" homes and fancy shops of Ocean Village can be forgiven a moist eye or two when remembering the days that used to be.

John Treasure Jones presided over the last voyages of no less than three liners — the Mauretenia, the Saxonia and the Queen Mary. No wonder they called him "Undertaker Jones"! The Mary's final trip, also its master's own, was a unique one for a transatlantic liner. Bought as a tourist attraction by the Californian city of Long Beach in 1967, she was too big for the Panama Canal and had to go "the long way". Its skipper

was thrilled at the prospect of rounding the Horn for the first time.

Yet all this nearly didn't happen. The 15-year-old Pembrokeshire farmer's son, drawn to the sea by the call of the blood (his maternal grandfather was a sailing ship skipper) and, he admits, by all the nice girls seeming to love a sailor, found his first trip in a rusty "tramp" so unpleasant that he was all for giving it up.

The shame of running home, though, made him bite the bullet, and once he got used to homesickness, seasickness, watches of four hours on and four hour off, and the terrible pay, John Treasure Jones, the lad whose second Christian name has an appropriately salty sea yarn ring to it, began to enjoy the life he was only to desert once.

This was during the Depression when the White Star Line, which he had joined after obtaining his master's ticket in June, 1929, dismissed all officers with less than 15 years' service. John found himself working on his dad's farm for a

Captain and Mrs. Treasure Jones on the bridge of the "Mary".

year, then got a job as an assistant superintendent stevedore in Liverpool before returning to sea in 1934 and joining Cunard White Star two years later.

A peacetime reservist, John served in the Royal Navy during the war and survived one of several narrow squeaks when the ship in which he was navigator was torpedoed — he was four hours on a raft before being picked up. He ended the war with the rank of captain.

Rejoining Cunard in 1947, John Treasure Jones was appointed staff captain of the Queen Mary and, except for the odd voyage in a couple of other liners, remained in that capacity until he was appointed in command of the Media in May, 1957. From that date, until he delivered the Queen Mary to Long Beach on December 8, 1967, he commanded the Sylvania, Saxonia, Carinthia, Mauretania, the Queen Elizabeth and, from December 30, 1965, the Mary.

He once told a reporter that he saw his job as a liner's master as one of many parts — "PRO, chairman of a large hotel complex, even vicar!" (he conducted the Sunday service but never gave a sermon . . .). But though he enjoyed the job immensely, after 47 years at sea he adjusted well to retirement and a landlubber's life. At 83 in 1989 he was still golfing, though he gave up playing cricket when he was 80! Like his fellow ex-skippers of the Queens, Donald MacLean, who went to live at Warsash, and Geoffrey Marr, who chose Downton, Captain Treasure Jones resides outside the city — at Chandler's Ford.

Looking back, he sees one of his greatest thrills as taking the Mauretania into his home port of Milford Haven for the opening by the Queen

This historic picture, taken in 1946, the year before John Treasure Jones rejoined Cunard, shows the Queen Elizabeth, newly fitted out for her trials, being passed in Southampton Docks by the Queen Mary (right) — she was returning from war service as a troopship. (Photos: Southern Newspapers).

Mother of an oil terminal. He reckons that quite a few people turned out to see the local boy who had made good — in 1968, by the way, the land of his fathers honoured the captain when the Duke of Edinburgh presented him with an honorary doctorate in law at the University of Wales in Cardiff. But nothing in the life of John Treasure Jones could quite compare with the epic final voyage — 1,500 miles in 39 days — to Long Beach. With him on that most memorable of trips was his proud wife Belle (they have three sons and a daughter).

Financial problems have dogged the Long Beach enterprise and the maritime museum idea has never seen fruition, but Captain Treasure Jones was hopeful that the new master lessees, Disneyland, would be able to give his old ship literally a new lease of life. Since he handed her over he has been back several times, the last occasion in 1986 for the 50th anniversary of her maiden voyage.

It's nice to keep in touch with your old ship. . . .

The Verne Sisters

Adela Verne was the best-known of the three musical sisters whose home in Southampton's Portland Street is marked by a commemorative plaque. She was the youngest of the ten children of a German couple who changed their name to Verne from the less attractive Wurm.

The former Herr Wurm, a music teacher and the organist at St Joseph's Roman Catholic Church in Bugle Street, fathered four daughters who became pre-eminent in music. There was the eldest, Marie, better known in Germany as a pianist and composer and who kept the name Wurm; there was Mathilde, who deserted the concert platform to teach and included among her pupils our present Queen Mother; and there was composer Alice (remembered with Adela and Mathilde on the plaque).

It was Adela, though, who made the most impact on the world of music. Born in Portland Street in 1877, her career spanned a remarkable era. She gave her first recital in Southampton at the age of four playing a Bach fugue, made her debut at Crystal Palace at 14, and shortly before her death at 74 gave the first television performance of Mozart's two-piano concerto with her son, John Vallier.

Taught initially by her sisters Alice and Mathilde and later by Paderewski, who called her "one of the world's greatest pianists," Adela toured America, Canada, Mexico, Australia and all over Europe, and was acclaimed wherever she went. Saint-Saens called her "a great artist."

She was the first pianist in this country to give a solo recital at the Albert Hall, the first to play Brahms' B Flat Piano Concerto at the "Proms", and the first to play Cesar Frank's Symphonic

Adela Verne

Variations in England. She toured with Melba, Tetrazzini, Ysaye, Clare Butt.

And right up until the end she is said to have played magnificently. Her last appearance was at Wigmore Hall shortly before her death in 1952. Musicologist Arthur Hedley, writing in the programme for a commemorative concert, wrote: "No-one who had the privilege of knowing Adela Verne and of hearing her at the height of her powers is likely to question her right to be regarded as the finest woman pianist of her generation."

Alice was the most exceptional sister as a composer. Sir Malcolm Sargent conducted a performance of her most important work, the Mass in B Flat. She also wrote a pianoforte trio, a quartet, a quintet and suites, and in her 1950 Adagio for

Strings is said to have revealed a contemporary outlook hitherto missing from her compositions.

Mathilde, born in 1865, was the great teacher — founder of the Mathilde Verne Pianoforte College in London's Cromwell Road where the ten-year-old Lady Elizabeth Bowes-Lyon, our Queen Mother, had her first piano lesson. She and her brother David evidently made great progress in just two terms without any prior knowledge of music. Mathilde herself had a famous teacher — Clara Schumann, who had also heard the six-year-old Adela and wanted to take her, too, but the little girl was much too young to leave home for Frankfurt.

"Plain, old-fashioned heart," a concentration on a deep and simple emotion not to be confused with sentimentality, was the quality which Mathilde felt should be singled out as the one to be cultivated with young musicians. She had remarkable success with her theory — this was the woman who discovered and trained the great Solomon.

The role of her parents in the girls' success almost goes without saying. Not only was their father, John Evangelist Verne, a music teacher; so was their mother, Sophie (whose sister, incidentally, was the mother of a famous artist from Southampton, Sir Hubert Herkomer).

The Vernes were by no means well-off — father only earned £20 a year at St Joseph's and almost all of this went on the rent of their Portland Street home where they lived from 1866 to 1892. To make ends meet John Verne and his wife taught for many hours daily . . . with their daughters among the pupils.

How proud they would be to read the Portland Street plaque commemorating Mathilde, Alice and Adela "who achieved great distinction and world fame as pianists, teachers of the pianoforte and composers". . . .

The Verne sisters' commemorative plaque on the wall of their former Portland Street home.

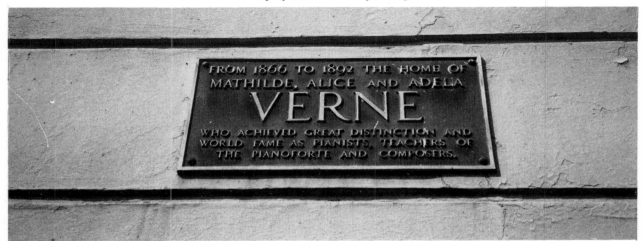

Isaac Watts

Isaac Watts: this portrait in Tudor House Museum is on loan from the National Portrait Gallery.

Four times an hour the chimes of *Our God Our Help in Ages Past* ring out from Southampton's Civic Centre clock tower. Across Commercial Road, in West Park (often popularly called Watts Park), stands a statue put up in 1861 to commemorate the writer of this and so many other famous hymns sung every Sunday throughout the earth — Isaac Watts, father of English hymnody.

There are other local memorials to this son of the city. In Winchester Road at the junction with Luccombe Road stands the Isaac Watts Memorial Church. At the Parish Church of the Ascension in Bitterne Park, noteworthy for its beautiful stained glass, are four memorial windows illustrating Watts' hymns, and the United Reformed Church in Brunswick Place has a sculptured head and shoulders of the hymnwriter which were saved from the blitzed ruins of the Above Bar Congregational Church — a building with close Watts family connections.

A plaque opposite the rear of Marks and Spencer's store in Vincent's Walk records the site of the Watts Memorial Hall, built in 1875-76. Like the church and the Watts family home in French Street, this suffered enemy action in the Second World War.

Deservedly, then, Isaac Watts is generously recognised in his native town. Less so, however, in some other quarters. The writer of such "hits" as *When I Survey the Wondrous Cross, There is a Land of Pure Delight* and *Jesus Shall Reign Where'er the Sun* turned up recently in Nicholas T. Parsons' study *The Joy of Bad Verse* (Collins) . . . and in 1974 Southampton MP Richard Mitchell failed in his attempt to have a special stamp issued to commemorate the 300th anniversary of Isaac's birth.

Isaac was born in the Above Bar Street house which became the first meeting place of the Above Bar Church, though the family soon moved to French Street. Watts' father, also christened Isaac, had been jailed twice for his beliefs, but the climate of religious tolerance improved in 1688 with the Declaration in Indulgence, and Isaac Senior became a deacon in the new Congregational Church in Above Bar.

Intolerance continued to flower, however, for when a prominent townsman offered to pay for an Oxford education for bright young Isaac, the lad had to turn the offer down — it would have meant renouncing his nonconformist beliefs.

The child prodigy who began learning Latin from his father at the age of four went to the Free Grammar School, which eventually became King Edward VI School, before moving on to South

His greatest hits are still sung throughout the world

Newington Academy. At King Edward's he turned out Latin verses, and Stoke Newington saw his first lyrics in English.

His first religious poems were, as Southampton journalist Gordon Sewell put it, "expressions of the mood of the spirit." Hymnwriting came a little later. The two years he spent in the family home after leaving college saw the young Isaac studying church history, the psalms and the hymns of the Dissenter writers.

"Write something better," advised Isaac Senior when his son complained about the quality of the metrical psalms sung at the meeting house. So, the story goes, Isaac Watts sat down and composed a hymn still sung wherever Protestants hold their services — *Behold the Glories of the Lamb.*

That would have been in the 1690s, when some of his later famous hymns were sung for the first time at the Congregational Church in Above Bar. After a period as a tutor to the family of Sir

The Isaac Watts Memorial Church in Winchester Road shortly after completion. Photo: Southern Newspapers Ltd.

John Hartopp at Stoke Newington, Isaac became pastor of a London Congregational Church, his fame as a preacher, author and hymnwriter spreading gradually as years went by. He died in 1748.

Though the words of this Puritan divine, born in the year Milton died, still divide the critics, they live on. Generations of parents have admonished their children with such lines as *Satin finds some mischief still for idle hands to do,* or the admonitory *How doth the little busy bee improve each shining hour.*

His infelicities, though, are pounced on still. Parsons quotes from *On the Death of Mrs. Mary Peacock: Hark! She bids all her friends adieu,/ Our eyes the radiant saint pursue/ Through liquid telescopes of tears.* Or how about: *Not all the gay pageants that breathe/ Can with a dead body compare?*

Watts' visions of God's wrath are unpalatable today. Take this: *There is a dreadful Hell/ And Everlasting pains;/ There sinners must with devils dwell/ In darkness, fire and chains.* Or: *But lips that dare to be so profane/ To mock, and jeer, and scoff/ At holy things and holy men/ The Lord shall cut them off.* The doctor goes on to recall God's response to the children who baited old Elisha: *God quickly stopp'd their wicked breath,/ And sent two raging bears/ That tore them limb from limb to death/ With blood, and groans, and tears.*

Nasty! But the best of Watts is splendid, as one great writer of lyrics, A. E. Housman, recognised. Can there ever have been a greater expression of eternity than this: *A thousand ages in Thy sight/ Are like an evening gone; Short as the watch that ends the night/ Before the rising sun?*

BIBLIOGRAPHY

Jane Austen's England: Maggie Lane (Hale, 1986); Southampton's Heavyweight Champion: John Murphy (Hampshire, September 1986 issue); Martin Bell: Complete Poems edited by Peter Porter (Bloodaxe Books, 1988); Philip Brannon, 1817-1890; Dr. A. T. Markwick (Proceedings of the Hampshire Field Club and Archaeological Society, Vol. 45, 1989); Memoirs of the Comte de Cartrie (John Lane, 1906); F. L. Bridell, 1830-1863: John Sweetman (Southampton Art Gallery Catalogue Series); Herbert Collins, 1885-1975, Architect and Worker for Peace: Robert Williams (Paul Cave Publications, Ltd and the City of Southampton Society, 1985); The Prostitutes' Padre: Tom Cullen (The Bodley Head, 1975); Suffragettes, Suffragists and Party Politics in Southampton, 1907-14: Pamela Johnston (Hampshire Field Club and Archaeological Society Proceedings, August 1983); Georgia On My Mind — the Nat Gonella Story: Ron Brown in conjunction with Cyril Brown (Milestone Publications, 1985); Gordon's Southampton Home: A. G. K. Leonard (Hampshire, June 1981); Eminent Victorians: Lytton Strachey (Chatto & Windus, 1918); Memorials and Mementoes of General Gordon: A. G. K. Leonard (Hampshire, January 1985); Maundy Gregory — Purveyor of Honours: Tom Cullen (the Bodley Head, 1974); Hartleyana; Alexander Anderson (Scottish Academic Press and Southampton University Press, 1987); Gordon Craig — The Story of His Life: Edward Craig (Gollancz, 1968); Victorian Olympus: William Grant (Jonathan Cape, 1952); The Benny Hill Story: John Smith (W. H. Allen, 1988); Hampshire's Own Admiral: Eric Wyeth Gadd (Hampshire, November 1983); Southampton — The English Gateway: Bernard Knowles (Hutchinson, 1951); The Buildings of England: Hampshire and the Isle of Wight: Nikolaus Pevsner and David Lloyd (Penguin, 1967); R. J. Mitchell: Dr. Gordon Mitchell and others (Nelson and Saunders, 1986); The Youngest Son: Ivor Montagu (Lawrence and Wishart, 1970); From Bitterne Park to Broadway: The Story of Stanley Ridges: John Edgar Mann (Hampshire, April, 1986); Argentina's First Dictator: John Godwin (London Evening News, September 21, 1956); An Appailing Talent: John Baxter (Michael Joseph, 1973); William Shayer — 200th birthday of Hampshire's Great Artist: Brian Stewart and Mervyn Cutten (Hampshire, June 1987); Wiltshire's General Shrapnel: "A Correspondent" (Bath & Wilts Evening Chronicle, September 12, 1961); His Invention Helped to Win the Battle of Waterloo: S. M. Gifford (Bath & Wilts Evening Chronicle, June 17, 1965); Stories of Southampton Streets: A. G. K. Leonard (Paul Cave Publications, 1984); The Joy of Bad Verse: Nicholas T. Parsons (Collins, 1988); Monuments and Memorials in Southampton: Robert Douch (City of Southampton, 1968).